# Undergraduate Texts in Mathematics

*Editors*

F. W. Gehring
P. R. Halmos

# Undergraduate Texts in Mathematics

*(continued after Index)*

Louis Brickman

# Mathematical Introduction to Linear Programming and Game Theory

Springer-Verlag
New York  Berlin  Heidelberg
London  Paris  Tokyo

Louis Brickman
Department of Mathematics and Statistics
State University of New York at Albany
Albany, NY 12222
U.S.A.

Library of Congress Cataloging-in-Publication Data
Brickman, Louis.
    Mathematical introduction to linear programming and game theory
Louis Brickman.
        p.   cm.—(Undergraduate texts in mathematics)
    Bibliography: p.
    Includes index.
    ISBN 0-387-96931-4
    1. Linear programming.   2. Game theory.   I. Title.   II. Series.
T57.74.B74   1989
519.7′2—dc20                                                    89-11257
                                                               CIP

Typeset by Asco Trade Typesetting Ltd., Hong Kong.
Printed and bound by R.R. Donnelley & Sons, Harrisonburg, Virginia.
Printed in the United States of America.

9 8 7 6 5 4 3 2 1

ISBN 0-387-96931-4 Springer-Verlag New York Berlin Heidelberg
ISBN 3-540-96931-4 Springer-Verlag Berlin Heidelberg New York

To Myra

# Preface

## Scope and Level

The principal objectives of this book are to define linear programming and its usefulness, to explain the operation and elementary theory of the simplex algorithm, to present duality theory in a simple fashion, and to give a well-motivated account of matrix games. The required mathematical tools, beyond arithmetic and high school algebra, are essentially limited to summation notation, basic language of sets and functions, and elementary notions of probability. Despite this technical simplicity, our subject has depth and subtlety. The author believes that a mathematically rigorous exposition is necessary to convey the underlying theory and, conversely, that learning the subject in this way will improve the student's understanding of mathematical reasoning. The exposition consists of definitions, theorems, proofs, discussions, and examples, interwoven in mature mathematical style. Such a treatment requires of the reader the sophistication to handle some abstraction, apply definitions literally, follow certain logical arguments, and profit from various remarks and examples. These abilities, as well as the more concrete tools listed above, could be acquired from prior courses in linear algebra, calculus, or probability theory. A few concepts from these subjects (transpose matrix, bounded function, expected value) are explained in this book when needed. The author has used preliminary versions of the book in his undergraduate classes. Almost all of the material can be covered in one semester.

## Chapter Notes and Summaries

Certain concepts concerning simultaneous linear equations (pivoting, equivalent systems, basic solution) are essential to the simplex algorithm. The exposition flows best if these concepts and a few theorems about them are made explicit in advance. Chapter 1 serves this function. In Chapter 2, linear programming (LP) is introduced, with the classical production problem and diet problem as motivating examples. Definitions are given for "LP problem," "primal form," "solving an LP problem," "objective function," "linear constraints," and other fundamental notions of LP. Then it is shown, in a precisely specified sense, that inequality constraints can be replaced by equations. This paves the way for applying the material of Chapter 1 and for introducing the simplex algorithm, denoted SIMPLEX.

The algorithm SIMPLEX is the subject of Chapter 3, which is the core of the book. The elegant *condensed tableau* is employed in this chapter and throughout the book. This tableau is easiest to pivot (after a little experience), requires the least amount of space and notational cluttering, and conveys all the essential information clearly. Many proofs are given in a condensed tableau format, in which they are readily grasped. Most important, condensed tableaux make duality theory almost transparent later in Chapter 5. In a certain specific sense, every LP problem is representable by a condensed tableau. If, in addition, all the right-hand constants are nonnegative, the tableau is called a *simplex tableau*. Problems representable by simplex tableaux are the ones to which SIMPLEX is directly applicable, and the ones studied in Chapter 3. The steps of SIMPLEX are motivated and justified, the stopping criteria (optimality and unboundedness patterns) are established, and the SIMPLEX flowchart is given. Finally, termination theorems and cycling are discussed. Bland's theorem is proved with a minimum of computation.

Chapter 4 begins with the observation that whenever a condensed tableau is pivoted, a closely related tableau, called the dual tableau, is automatically pivoted also. This fact is then used to prove that a simple-to-define pivoting algorithm will transform any condensed tableau with one or more negative right-hand constants into either a simplex tableau or a tableau showing that the underlying LP problem is infeasible. In the first case the solution can be completed by SIMPLEX. It then follows that every LP problem can be solved in one or two "phases" by pivoting. The chapter concludes with a couple of refinements of the indicated *phase I* algorithm. One of these refinements is the *dual simplex* algorithm.

In Chapter 5 the production problem and a closely related "entrepreneur's problem" are used to introduce dual LP problems. It follows easily from the definition given that dual LP problems are representable by dual tableaux. The results of Chapter 4 and, therefore, a simple "geometric" proof of the important duality theorem are then available. The theorem asserts, roughly put, that solving any LP problem automatically solves the problem with which it is paired. Chapter 5 applications of the duality theorem include a joint-outcomes chart for dual LP problems, a proof of the complementary slackness theorem, and a discussion of *marginal values* (*shadow prices*).

Chapter 6, the final chapter, treats matrix games. The following questions are the subject of considerable informal discussion: What are the goals of the two players? Why should they make their choices randomly? What is conservative play and what is the alternative? Such discussion motivates the introduction of "mixed strategies" and helps to illuminate the fundamental theorem of matrix games. The theorem is illustrated by several examples and by "saddle entries," and finally proved by duality theory. The exact role of the LP problem used to analyze a matrix game is determined.

There are problems to be worked at the end of each chapter. Doing so will enhance the student's understanding of the theory, develop the necessary computational skills, and sharpen mathematical reasoning. Also, some of the problems significantly extend the treatment in the text.

### Acknowledgments

I am grateful to George Martin, Richard O'Neil, Myra Brickman, and David Brickman for valuable suggestions concerning substance or style; to Susan Brickman for the clever names of the game players in Chapter 6; to JoAnna Aveyard for her excellent typing of most of the manuscript; to Ellen Fisher and Judith Brickman for ably typing the remaining parts; and to the Department of Mathematics and Statistics at the State University of New York at Albany for the use of its resources and for the privilege of teaching Linear Programming and Game Theory throughout the entire writing of the book. Finally, there was one contribution for which no substitute could have existed. My wife, Myra, created the environment that fostered writing. This book is dedicated to her with my deepest gratitude.

*Albany*                                                                 LOUIS BRICKMAN
*August 1988*

# Contents

# CHAPTER 1

# Simultaneous Linear Equations

In order to establish notation, we begin by describing the most general system of simultaneous linear equations. Explanations and many examples come immediately afterward. Let $m$ and $n$ be positive integers, and let us consider the following system of $m$ equations in $n$ *variables* $x_1, x_2, \ldots, x_n$:

$$
\begin{cases}
a_{11}x_1 + a_{12}x_2 + \cdots + a_{1n}x_n = b_1, \\
a_{21}x_1 + a_{22}x_2 + \cdots + a_{2n}x_n = b_2, \\
\quad\vdots \qquad\quad \vdots \qquad\quad \vdots \qquad \vdots \qquad\quad \vdots \\
a_{m1}x_1 + a_{m2}x_2 + \cdots + a_{mn}x_n = b_m.
\end{cases}
\tag{1}
$$

The *coefficients* $a_{11}, a_{12}$, and so on, are distinguished by double subscripts, the first giving the equation number, and the second indicating the variable being multiplied. We shall refer to $b_1, \ldots, b_m$ as the *constants* of system (1). All coefficients and constants are assumed to be real numbers, as are the values sought for the variables $x_1, \ldots, x_n$.

We shall almost always have $2 \leq m < n$, so that the smallest system likely to be considered would have the form

$$
\begin{cases}
a_{11}x_1 + a_{12}x_2 + a_{13}x_3 = b_1, \\
a_{21}x_1 + a_{22}x_2 + a_{23}x_3 = b_2.
\end{cases}
$$

Specializing further, we consider the system

$$
\begin{cases}
2x_1 - 3x_2 + 4x_3 = 0, \\
\phantom{2}x_1 + \phantom{3}x_2 \phantom{{}+ 4x_3} = 7.
\end{cases}
\tag{2}
$$

Here $a_{11} = 2, a_{12} = -3, a_{13} = 4, a_{21} = 1, a_{22} = 1, a_{23} = 0, b_1 = 0$, and $b_2 = 7$. The *ordered triple* $(1, 6, 4)$ is called a *solution* of system (2) because if 1, 6, and 4 are substituted for $x_1, x_2$, and $x_3$, respectively, then both (all) equations of the system are satisfied. Indeed,

$$\begin{cases} 2(1) - 3(6) + 4(4) = 0, \\ \quad 1 + 6 \qquad\qquad = 7. \end{cases}$$

The word "equation" is used both for variable expressions such as $2x_1 - 3x_2 + 4x_3 = 0$, and also for numerical expressions, for instance, $2(1) - 3(6) + 4(4) = 0$. There is, however, a fundamental difference: The latter happens to be true, whereas the former is neither true nor false; the expression $2x_1 - 3x_2 + 4x_3 = 0$ becomes capable of truth or falsity only after the variables $x_1$, $x_2$, and $x_3$ are replaced by numbers.

We remark without proof that a system of simultaneous linear equations with fewer equations than variables ($m < n$) never has a unique solution. For instance, besides $(1, 6, 4)$, the reader can easily check that $(0, 7, \frac{21}{4})$ and $(7, 0, -\frac{7}{2})$ are solutions of (2). The reader should therefore learn to say "*a* solution," not "*the* solution." It can be shown that linear systems with $m < n$ either have no solution or infinitely many solutions. Later in the chapter we shall determine all the infinitely many solutions of (2). An example of a system with no solution is

$$\begin{cases} x_1 + x_2 + x_3 = 11, \\ 2x_1 + 2x_2 + 2x_3 = 23. \end{cases}$$

This assertion can easily be proved by assuming the existence of a solution $(s_1, s_2, s_3)$ and then using simple algebra to reach a contradiction. Such a system is called *inconsistent*.

Let us now define *solution* formally.

**Definition 1.** An $n$-tuple of real numbers $(s_1, \ldots, s_n)$ is a *solution* of system (1) if it satisfies all the equations of (1), that is, if

$$\begin{cases} a_{11}s_1 + a_{12}s_2 + \cdots + a_{1n}s_n = b_1, \\ a_{21}s_1 + a_{22}s_2 + \cdots + a_{2n}s_n = b_2, \\ \quad\vdots \qquad\quad \vdots \qquad\quad \vdots \qquad \vdots \qquad \vdots \\ a_{m1}s_1 + a_{m2}s_2 + \cdots + a_{mn}s_n = b_m. \end{cases}$$

The set of all such $n$-tuples is called the *solution set* of (1).

It is important to realize that $s_1, \ldots, s_n$ are *numbers* and that the $m$ equations just written are true statements. On the other hand, $x_1, \ldots, x_n$ are *variables*, and the equations in (1) are neither true nor false.

The next important definition is that of *equivalence* of two systems.

**Definition 2.** Two systems of equations with the same variables are *equivalent* if every solution of either system is also a solution of the other system. In other words, both systems have the same solution set.

An example of two equivalent systems is (2) and the following system, denoted (2′).

$$\begin{cases} 2x_1 - 3x_2 + 4x_3 = 0, \\ x_1 + x_2 = 7, \\ 3x_1 - 2x_2 + 4x_3 = 7. \end{cases} \tag{2'}$$

The first two equations of (2′) are the same as those of (2), and the third equation is the sum of the first two equations. To prove equivalence, let $(s_1, s_2, s_3)$ be an arbitrary solution of (2). Then we have the (true) equations

$$\begin{cases} 2s_1 - 3s_2 + 4s_3 = 0, \\ s_1 + s_2 = 7. \end{cases}$$

Adding these equations, we obtain

$$3s_1 - 2s_2 + 4s_3 = 7.$$

Thus, all the equations of (2′) become true when $s_1, s_2, s_3$ are substituted for $x_1, x_2, x_3$, respectively. This means, by definition, that $(s_1, s_2, s_3)$ is a solution of (2′). Conversely, let $(t_1, t_2, t_3)$ be an arbitrary solution of (2′). Then all three equations of (2′) are true when $x_1 = t_1, x_2 = t_2, x_3 = t_3$. In particular, the first two equations become true. Thus, $(t_1, t_2, t_3)$ is a solution of (2), and the equivalence of (2) and (2′) has been established.

Another system equivalent to (2) is

$$\begin{cases} x_1 - \frac{3}{2}x_2 + 2x_3 = 0, \\ x_1 + x_2 = 7. \end{cases} \tag{2''}$$

Here the first equation is obtained by multiplying the first equation of (2) by $\frac{1}{2}$, and the second equation is identical to that of (2). If $(t_1, t_2, t_3)$ is an arbitrary solution of (2″), we have the equations

$$\begin{cases} t_1 - \frac{3}{2}t_2 + 2t_3 = 0, \\ t_1 + t_2 = 7. \end{cases}$$

Multiplying the first of these by 2, the reciprocal of $\frac{1}{2}$, we obtain

$$\begin{cases} 2t_1 - 3t_2 + 4t_3 = 0, \\ t_1 + t_2 = 7. \end{cases}$$

Thus $(t_1, t_2, t_3)$ is a solution of (2). Similarly, it is easy to see that any solution of (2) must also be a solution of (2″). Hence (2) and (2″) are equivalent, as asserted. Instead of multiplying by $\frac{1}{2}$ to get system (2″) from (2), we could have used any multiplier except 0, and an equivalent system would have resulted. If 0 had been used, the new system would have been

$$\begin{cases} 0x_1 + 0x_2 + 0x_3 = 0, \\ x_1 + x_2 = 7. \end{cases}$$

This system is not equivalent to (2) because (1, 6, 0), for example, is a solution here, but not of (2). Incidentally, since (2) is equivalent to both (2′) and (2″), it follows that (2′) and (2″) are equivalent. This is a special case of the following simple theorem, which we record for repeated future use. We omit the easy proof. (Equivalent systems have equal solution sets.)

**Theorem 1.** *Let $S_1$, $S_2$, ..., $S_m$ ($m \geq 3$) be systems of simultaneous linear equations, and let $S_r$ be equivalent to $S_{r+1}$ for $r = 1, ..., m-1$. Then $S_1$ is equivalent to $S_m$.*

Next we state a very useful theorem that describes two equivalence-preserving operations for linear systems of equations. (Manipulating equations that are neither true nor false, maintaining equivalence all the while, is an undertaking that is best guided by a theorem.) The notation in the theorem saves much writing. Also, it shows that the theorem is valid even for systems of "nonlinear" equations, that is, systems not of form (1).

**Theorem 2.** *Each of the following operations on a system of simultaneous linear equations produces an equivalent system:*
(i) *Replace any equation of the system by any nonzero constant multiple of itself, and keep the other equations intact.*
(ii) *Denoting the equations by*

$$f_1(x_1, ..., x_n) = b_1, ..., f_m(x_1, ..., x_n) = b_m,$$

*or more briefly $f_1 = b_1, ..., f_m = b_m$, choose any two equations, $f_r = b_r$ and $f_i = b_i$, and any number c. Replace $f_i = b_i$ by*

$$f_i + cf_r = b_i + cb_r$$

*(add c times the rth equation to the ith equation). All other equations, including $f_r = b_r$, remain unchanged.*

*Proof.* The idea of the proof for (i) occurred in our discussion of the equivalence of (2) and (2''); the key is that any nonzero number has a reciprocal. Let us therefore turn to operation (ii). We denote the original system $f_1 = b_1, ...,$ $f_m = b_m$ by (1) and the modified system by (1'). Suppose $(s_1, ..., s_n)$ is a solution of (1). Then $f_1(s_1, ..., s_n) = b_1, ..., f_m(s_1, ..., s_n) = b_m$. In particular, $f_r(s_1, ..., s_n) = b_r$ and $f_i(s_1, ..., s_n) = b_i$. Therefore $cf_r(s_1, ..., s_n) = cb_r$, and by addition we obtain

$$f_i(s_1, ..., s_n) + cf_r(s_1, ..., s_n) = b_i + cb_r.$$

In other words, the equation

$$f_i(x_1, ..., x_n) + cf_r(x_1, ..., x_n) = b_i + cb_r$$

of (1') becomes correct for $x_1 = s_1, ..., x_n = s_n$. All other equations of (1') also occur in (1). These, therefore, are also satisfied for $x_1 = s_1, ..., x_n = s_n$. Thus, any solution $(s_1, ..., s_n)$ of (1) is also a solution of (1').

Conversely, let $(t_1, ..., t_n)$ be an arbitrary solution of (1'). In particular, $f_r(t_1, ..., t_n) = b_r$ and $f_i(t_1, ..., t_n) + cf_r(t_1, ..., t_n) = b_i + cb_r$. Multiplying the first of these equations by $c$ and subtracting from the other, we obtain $f_i(t_1, ..., t_n) = b_i$. In other words, the equation $f_i(x_1, ..., x_n) = b_i$ of (1) becomes true for $x_1 = t_1, ..., x_n = t_n$. All other equations in (1) are also in (1') and hence are correct for $x_1 = t_1, ..., x_n = t_n$. Therefore, $(t_1, ..., t_n)$ is a solution of (1), and we conclude that (1) and (1') are equivalent.   $\square$

We make repeated use of Theorems 1 and 2 in the remainder of this chapter and later mainly in the simplex algorithm. Let us illustrate the use of (i) and (ii) in producing equivalent systems beginning with

$$\begin{cases} \boxed{2x_1} - 3x_2 + 4x_3 = 0, \\ x_1 + x_2 \quad\quad = 7. \end{cases} \tag{2}$$

At the same time we circle the term $2x_1$ and introduce the notion of *pivoting*. We first use (i) to multiply the first equation of system (2) by $\frac{1}{2}$. This produces coefficient 1 in the *pivot term* and leads to the system

$$\begin{cases} x_1 - \frac{3}{2}x_2 + 2x_3 = 0, \\ x_1 + x_2 \quad\quad = 7. \end{cases} \tag{2''}$$

We now wish to eliminate $x_1$ from every equation (just one equation this time) except the pivot equation. Using (ii), we multiply the first equation by $(-1)$ and add the resulting equation to the second. This eliminates $x_1$ in the second equation and produces the equivalent system

$$\begin{cases} x_1 - \frac{3}{2}x_2 + 2x_3 = 0, \\ \boxed{\frac{5}{2}x_2} - 2x_3 = 7. \end{cases}$$

Finally, we choose $\frac{5}{2}x_2$ as the pivot term, multiply the second equation by $\frac{2}{5}$ (yielding $x_2 - \frac{4}{5}x_3 = \frac{14}{5}$), multiply this new equation (mentally) by $\frac{3}{2}$, and add the result (physically) to the previous top equation. All this leads to the system

$$\begin{cases} x_1 \quad\quad + \frac{4}{5}x_3 = \frac{21}{5}, \\ x_2 - \frac{4}{5}x_3 = \frac{14}{5}. \end{cases} \tag{2'''}$$

We have now reached a system having a special form, which we shall define and exploit shortly. First we define "pivoting" formally and state its basic properties as Theorem 3.

**Definition 3.** In a linear system of simultaneous equations, $f_1 = b_1, \ldots, f_m = b_m$, let $a_{rs}$ be the coefficient of $x_s$ in the equation $f_r = b_r$, and let $a_{rs} \neq 0$. Then *pivoting at* $a_{rs}$ consists of the following sequence of operations:

(i) Replace the equation $f_r = b_r$ by $a_{rs}^{-1} f_r = a_{rs}^{-1} b_r$.
(ii) For every $i \neq r$, replace the $i$th equation, $f_i = b_i$, by

$$f_i - \frac{a_{is}}{a_{rs}} f_r = b_i - \frac{a_{is}}{a_{rs}} b_r.$$

(Here $a_{is}$ is the coefficient of $x_s$ in the $i$th equation.) For this sequence of operations the coefficient $a_{rs}$ is called the *pivot* or the *pivot coefficient*.

**Theorem 3.** *The system obtained by pivoting at $a_{rs}$ as described is equivalent to the original system. Moreover, in the new system the coefficient of $x_s$ is 1 in the equation replacing $f_r = b_r$, and 0 in every other equation.*

*Proof.* By Theorem 2 each operation involved in pivoting preserves equivalence. Thus the equivalence assertion above follows from Theorem 1. It is clear from (i) of Definition 3 that the coefficient of $x_s$ in the $r$th equation of the new system is 1. The rest follows from a study of (ii). We leave this to the reader and consider the proof complete.   □

Let us now return to system $(2''')$. The equations of $(2''')$ are all but solved for $x_1$ and $x_2$ in terms of $x_3$, and the system is said to be in $\{x_1, x_2\}$-*basic form*. We also say that $x_1$ and $x_2$ are the *basic variables*, whereas $x_3$ is called *nonbasic*. In larger systems there can, of course, be several nonbasic variables. Suppose now that $(s_1, s_2, s_3)$ is an arbitrary solution of $(2''')$. Then

$$s_1 = \tfrac{21}{5} - \tfrac{4}{5}s_3, \qquad s_2 = \tfrac{14}{5} + \tfrac{4}{5}s_3,$$

or equivalently,

$$(s_1, s_2, s_3) = (\tfrac{21}{5} - \tfrac{4}{5}s_3, \tfrac{14}{5} + \tfrac{4}{5}s_3, s_3).$$

Conversely, if $s_3$ is an arbitrary real number, direct substitution shows that such an ordered triple is a solution of $(2''')$. Thus, the infinity of such ordered triples is the complete solution set of $(2''')$. (Similarly, it will be clear that one can immediately write down all the solutions of any system in basic form. See Problem 2 at the end of the chapter.) Furthermore, since (2) and $(2''')$ are equivalent, *we have also found all the solutions of* (2). The special solution obtained by letting the nonbasic variable $x_3$ have the value 0 is $(\tfrac{21}{5}, \tfrac{14}{5}, 0)$. This solution is called the *basic solution* or, if greater clarity is needed, the $\{x_1, x_2\}$-basic solution. In a basic solution every nonbasic variable is given the value 0; this forces the value of each basic variable to be the constant on the right-hand side of the appropriate equation. We shall find that basic solutions play a crucial role in linear programming.

Let us now make formal definitions concerning basic form. For this it will be convenient to denote the number of equations by $m$ and the number of variables by $m + p$. The notation following is somewhat heavy, but subsequent examples will promote understanding.

**Definition 4.** We suppose that $m \geq 2$ and $p \geq 1$. Let $S$ be a system of $m$ linear equations in $m + p$ variables $x_1, \ldots, x_{m+p}$. Let $j_1, \ldots, j_m$ be distinct numbers from the set of subscripts $\{1, 2, \ldots, m + p\}$, and let $k_1, \ldots, k_p$ be the remaining elements. Then $S$ is in $\{x_{j_1}, \ldots, x_{j_m}\}$-*basic form* if the equations of $S$ can be written in the following form (where, for the first time, the order of terms is not dictated by the natural ordering of the subscripts of the variables):

$$
\begin{cases}
x_{j_1} + \displaystyle\sum_{q=1}^{p} \alpha_{1q} x_{k_q} = \beta_1, \\
\ \vdots \qquad \vdots \quad \ \ \vdots \qquad \vdots \\
x_{j_m} + \displaystyle\sum_{q=1}^{p} \alpha_{mq} x_{k_q} = \beta_m.
\end{cases}
\tag{3}
$$

[The equations $m + p = n$ and $\alpha_{iq} = a_{ik_q}$ reconcile some of the notation of (1) and (3).] We also say that $x_{j_1}, \ldots, x_{j_m}$ are *basic* variables or that $\{x_{j_1}, \ldots, x_{j_m}\}$ is a *basis* for $S$. The variables $x_{k_1}, \ldots, x_{k_p}$ not in the basis are then called *nonbasic* variables. We shall say simply that $S$ is in *basic form* if $S$ has some unspecified basis.

For a second example of basic form, we consider the system

$$\begin{cases} 3x_1 + x_2 - x_3 & = 2, \\ 2x_1 \phantom{+ x_2} + 3x_3 \phantom{+ x_3} + x_5 = 0, \\ x_1 \phantom{+ x_2 + 3x_3} + x_4 \phantom{+ x_5} = 7. \end{cases}$$

In the notation of Definition 4, we have $m = 3$, $p = 2$. Let $\{j_1, j_2, j_3\} = \{2, 5, 4\}$, and $\{k_1, k_2\} = \{1, 3\}$. Changing the order of addition in the three equations, we can write

$$\begin{cases} x_2 + 3x_1 - x_3 = 2, \\ x_5 + 2x_1 + 3x_3 = 0, \\ x_4 + x_1 \phantom{+ 3x_3} = 7. \end{cases}$$

It is now completely clear that the structure is a special case of (3) and that $\{x_2, x_5, x_4\}$ is a basis.

Instead of (3), a verbal description of a system in $\{x_{j_1}, \ldots, x_{j_m}\}$-basic form can be given: Each of the variables $x_{j_1}, \ldots, x_{j_m}$ has coefficient 1 in one equation of the system and coefficient 0 in every other equation. Conversely, in each equation of the system one of the variables $x_{j_1}, \ldots, x_{j_m}$ has coefficient 1 while all the others have coefficient 0.

In the example

$$\begin{cases} x_2 - x_3 \phantom{+ x_4} = 2, \\ \phantom{x_1} 3x_3 \phantom{+ x_4} + x_5 = 0, \\ x_1 \phantom{+ 3x_3} + x_4 \phantom{+ x_5} = 7, \end{cases}$$

either $\{x_2, x_5, x_4\}$ or $\{x_2, x_5, x_1\}$ is a basis. We shall return to this example after the next theorem and definition. The proof of the theorem is clear from (3).

**Theorem 4.** *Any linear system in basic form has the following property. For each assignment of arbitrary real values to the nonbasic variables, there is one and only one solution of the system in which the nonbasic variables have these values. In particular, there is a unique solution in which each nonbasic variable has the value 0. The value of each basic variable is then the constant in the unique equation containing that variable.*

As a consequence of Theorem 4, the following definition is meaningful.

**Definition 5.** In a linear system with basis $\{x_{j_1}, \ldots, x_{j_m}\}$, the $\{x_{j_1}, \ldots, x_{j_m}\}$-*basic solution* or the *basic solution with respect to* $\{x_{j_1}, \ldots, x_{j_m}\}$ is that solution in which every variable other than $x_{j_1}, \ldots, x_{j_m}$ has the value 0. Less precisely, we say that a solution of a system is a *basic solution* if the system has a basis with respect to which the solution is the basic solution.

For example, for the system

$$\begin{cases} x_2 - x_3 && = 2, \\ & 3x_3 + x_5 = 0, \\ x_1 && + x_4 && = 7, \end{cases}$$

considered earlier, the $\{x_2, x_4, x_5\}$-basic solution is given by

$$x_1 = 0, \qquad x_3 = 0, \qquad x_2 = 2, \qquad x_4 = 7, \qquad x_5 = 0,$$

or formally,

$$(0, 2, 0, 7, 0).$$

On the other hand the $\{x_1, x_2, x_5\}$-basic solution is $(7, 2, 0, 0, 0)$. Note that a basic variable can have the value 0 in a basic solution; the latter is then called a *degenerate* basic solution. (Such solutions can be an annoyance in applications of the simplex algorithm of Chapter 3.)

The following theorem asserts a uniqueness property of basic form. The theorem is both generally interesting and relevant to linear programming.

**Theorem 5.** *If both of two equivalent systems are in basic form and both have the same basis, then the two systems are identical—except possibly for the order in which the equations are written and the order of the terms within the equations.*

*Proof.* Let us translate our assertion into symbols. Since (3) is a completely general system in basic form, we may assume that one of our two equivalent systems is (3). The other system, which we shall denote by (3'), must then also have $x_{j_1}, \ldots, x_{j_m}$ as basic variables and $x_{k_1}, \ldots, x_{k_p}$ as nonbasic variables. Let us, if necessary, rewrite the equations of (3') so that the order of the equations and of the terms corresponds to that of (3). Thus we write the equation containing $x_{j_1}$ first, that containing $x_{j_2}$ second, and so on; within each equation $x_{k_1}$ will precede $x_{k_2}$, and so on. Then (3') has the form

$$\begin{cases} x_{j_1} + \sum_{q=1}^{p} \alpha'_{1q} x_{k_q} = \beta'_1, \\ \vdots \quad \vdots \quad \vdots \quad \vdots \\ x_{j_m} + \sum_{q=1}^{p} \alpha'_{mq} x_{k_q} = \beta'_m. \end{cases} \tag{3'}$$

Having taken into account the exception noted in the statement of the theorem, we must now prove $\beta_i = \beta'_i$ and $\alpha_{is} = \alpha'_{is}$ for all $i$ and $s$ ($1 \le i \le m, 1 \le s \le p$).

Now, the $\{x_{j_1}, \ldots, x_{j_m}\}$-basic solution of (3) is given by

$$x_{k_1} = \cdots = x_{k_p} = 0; \qquad x_{j_1} = \beta_1, \ldots, x_{j_m} = \beta_m.$$

Since (3) and (3′) are assumed to be equivalent, this solution of (3) must also be a solution of (3′). Substituting these values of the variables into (3′), we obtain

$$\beta_1 = \beta_1',$$
$$\vdots$$
$$\beta_m = \beta_m'.$$

To finish the proof, we choose the integer $s$ arbitrarily, $1 \le s \le p$. Then the following assignment of values gives a (nonbasic) solution of (3):

$$x_{k_s} = 1, \qquad x_{k_q} = 0 \quad \text{for } q \ne s; \qquad x_{j_1} = \beta_1 - \alpha_{1s}, \ldots, x_{j_m} = \beta_m - \alpha_{ms}.$$

These values must also satisfy (3′). Substitution yields

$$\beta_1 - \alpha_{1s} + \alpha_{1s}' = \beta_1',$$
$$\vdots \qquad \vdots \qquad \vdots \qquad \vdots$$
$$\beta_m - \alpha_{ms} + \alpha_{ms}' = \beta_m'.$$

Hence

$$\alpha_{1s} = \alpha_{1s}',$$
$$\vdots$$
$$\alpha_{ms} = \alpha_{ms}',$$

as required.    □

The final topic of the chapter is a special tableau representation for systems in basic form. This representation will be quite convenient later on, when we shall need to pivot systems in basic form, changing repeatedly from one basis to another.

**Definition 6.** The *condensed tableau* representation of system (3) (the general system in basic form) is the following, also denoted (3):

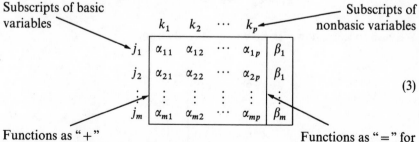

Subscripts of basic variables

Subscripts of nonbasic variables

(3)

Functions as "+" for every equation.

Functions as "=" for every equation.

Although we have used the definite article "the" in the phrase "the condensed tableau," any tableau differing from (3) by a permutation of the columns is equally acceptable provided that the column headings $k_1, \ldots, k_p$ are kept together with their columns. Such a difference between tableaux corresponds only to a difference in the order of addition in the linear system (3). We also accept a permutation of the rows of the tableau (3), row headings $j_1, \ldots, j_m$ staying with their rows. In constructing the condensed tableau (3), one places the subscripts of the basic variables along the left side of the tableau and those of the nonbasic variables across the top. The left edge of the tableau can be thought of as a plus sign for each of the $m$ equations. The vertical line separating the coefficients from the constants serves as an equal sign.

Let us illustrate Definition 6 by pairing two previously considered systems with their condensed tableau representations.

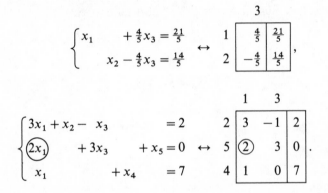

Let us also pivot the last system at 2 as indicated. (This takes $x_5$ out of the basis and replaces it by $x_1$.) We then pair the resulting system with a condensed tableau representation.

$$\begin{cases} x_2 - \tfrac{11}{2}x_3 & -\tfrac{3}{2}x_5 = 2 \\ x_1 & +\tfrac{3}{2}x_3 & +\tfrac{1}{2}x_5 = 0 \\ & -\tfrac{3}{2}x_3 + x_4 & -\tfrac{1}{2}x_5 = 7 \end{cases} \leftrightarrow \begin{array}{c|cc|c} & 5 & 3 & \\ \hline 2 & -\tfrac{3}{2} & -\tfrac{11}{2} & 2 \\ 1 & \tfrac{1}{2} & \tfrac{3}{2} & 0 \\ 4 & -\tfrac{1}{2} & -\tfrac{3}{2} & 7 \end{array}.$$

We wish to learn, however, how to go directly from

$$\begin{array}{c|cc|c} & 1 & 3 & \\ \hline 2 & 3 & -1 & 2 \\ 5 & ② & 3 & 0 \\ 4 & 1 & 0 & 7 \end{array} \tag{4}$$

to

$$
\begin{array}{c}
\phantom{2} \quad\; 5 \qquad 3 \\
\begin{array}{c|cc|c}
2 & -\frac{3}{2} & -\frac{11}{2} & 2 \\
1 & \frac{1}{2} & \frac{3}{2} & 0 \\
4 & -\frac{1}{2} & -\frac{3}{2} & 7
\end{array}
\end{array}
, \qquad (4')
$$

that is, how to pivot a condensed tableau. This is completely answered by the next theorem. The theorem will be extremely useful in future chapters.

**Theorem 6.** *Let the linear system with condensed tableau*

$$
\begin{array}{c}
\quad\; k_q \qquad\quad k_s \\
\begin{array}{c|ccccc|c}
 & \vdots & & \vdots & & & \vdots \\
j_r & \cdots\; \alpha_{rq}\; \cdots & & \boxed{\alpha_{rs}} & & \cdots & \beta_r \\
 & & & \vdots & & & \vdots \\
j_i & \cdots\; \alpha_{iq}\; \cdots & & \alpha_{is} & & \cdots & \beta_i \\
 & & & \vdots & & & \vdots
\end{array}
\end{array} \qquad (3)
$$

*be pivoted at $\alpha_{rs}$ ($\alpha_{rs} \neq 0$). Then the resulting system is again in basic form and represented by the tableau*

$$
\begin{array}{c}
\qquad\qquad k_q \qquad\qquad\qquad j_r \\
\begin{array}{c|ccc|c}
k_s & \cdots\; \dfrac{\alpha_{rq}}{\alpha_{rs}}\; \cdots & \cdots\; \dfrac{1}{\alpha_{rs}}\; \cdots & & \dfrac{\beta_r}{\alpha_{rs}} \\
 & & & & \\
j_i & \cdots\; \alpha_{iq} - \dfrac{\alpha_{is}\alpha_{rq}}{\alpha_{rs}}\; \cdots & \cdots\; -\dfrac{\alpha_{is}}{\alpha_{rs}}\; \cdots & & \beta_i - \dfrac{\alpha_{is}\beta_r}{\alpha_{rs}}
\end{array}
\end{array} . \qquad (3')
$$

[*We are determining the replacements, in (3'), of the following entries of (3): the pivot, any other coefficient in the pivot row, any other coefficient in the pivot column, an arbitrary coefficient in neither the pivot row nor the pivot column, the constant in the pivot row, and any other constant.*]

## MNEMONIC DIAGRAM

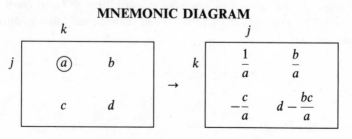

*Expressed verbally:*

(i)   *The pivot [in (3)] is replaced [in (3')] by its reciprocal (in the corresponding tableau position).*
(ii)  *The other elements in the pivot row (in (3)) are divided by the pivot (and the quotients placed in (3') in the corresponding positions).*
(iii) *The other elements in the pivot column (in (3)) are divided by the negative of the pivot.*
(iv)  *The pivot and any element in a different row and column lie at opposite corners of a rectangle [in (3), with sides parallel to those of (3)]. The replacement for any such element is*

$$itself - \frac{product\ of\ elements\ at\ other\ two\ corners}{pivot}.$$

(v)   *The numbers heading the row and column of the pivot are interchanged.*

*Proof.* The equation represented by the pivot row of (3) is

$$x_{j_r} + \sum_{q \neq s} \alpha_{rq} x_{k_q} + \alpha_{rs} x_{k_s} = \beta_r.$$

The first step (see Definition 3) in pivoting at $\alpha_{rs}$ is to divide this equation by $\alpha_{rs}$. This yields

$$x_{k_s} + \sum_{q \neq s} \frac{\alpha_{rq}}{\alpha_{rs}} x_{k_q} + \frac{1}{\alpha_{rs}} x_{j_r} = \frac{\beta_r}{\alpha_{rs}},$$

which is exactly the equation represented by the corresponding row of (3'). Next, for every $i \neq r$, we multiply the equation of the pivot row by $-\alpha_{is}/\alpha_{rs}$ and add the resulting equation to

$$x_{j_i} + \sum_{q \neq s} \alpha_{iq} x_{k_q} + \alpha_{is} x_{k_s} = \beta_i.$$

This eliminates $x_{k_s}$ and gives

$$x_{j_i} + \sum_{q \neq s} \left( \alpha_{iq} - \frac{\alpha_{is}\alpha_{rq}}{\alpha_{rs}} \right) x_{k_q} - \frac{\alpha_{is}}{\alpha_{rs}} x_{j_r} = \beta_i - \frac{\alpha_{is}\beta_r}{\alpha_{rs}}.$$

The appropriate row of (3') represents this equation, and the proof is complete.  □

We conclude the chapter by applying rules (i) through (v) to pivot (4) and obtain (4'). The workings of (i), (ii), (iii), and (v) are clear (do you agree?), so we illustrate only (iv):

$$-1 \to -1 - \frac{(3)(3)}{2} = -1 - \frac{9}{2} = -\frac{11}{2},$$

$$2 \to 2 - \frac{(0)(3)}{2} = 2,$$

$$0 \to 0 - \frac{(3)(1)}{2} = -\frac{3}{2},$$

$$7 \to 7 - \frac{(0)(1)}{2} = 7.$$

Condensed tableaux and our mechanical rules (i) through (v) for manipulating them are used extensively throughout the book. The reader will therefore eventually become proficient in the use of these rules. It is important, however, not to be become too mechanical: Keep in mind the system of equations represented by a given tableau, and remember that the five pivoting rules produce an equivalent system with a different basis.

PROBLEMS

1. Without using any theorems from the text, show that the system

$$\begin{cases} x_1 + 2x_2 - 4x_3 + x_4 = 3, \\ 2x_1 - 3x_2 + x_3 + 5x_4 = -4, \\ 7x_1 \qquad - 10x_3 + 13x_4 = 0, \end{cases}$$

has no solution.

*Suggestion*: Assume a solution, insert it into the system, and produce a contradiction.

2. Find all solutions of the system

$$\begin{cases} 2x_1 - x_2 + 2x_3 - x_4 + 3x_5 = 14, \\ x_1 + 2x_2 + 3x_3 + x_4 \qquad = 5, \\ x_1 \qquad - 2x_3 \qquad - 2x_5 = -10, \end{cases}$$

by first constructing an equivalent system with basis $\{x_2, x_4, x_1\}$. Also find the $\{x_2, x_4, x_1\}$-basic solution.

*Answer*: $(-10 + 2s + 2t, 49 - 11s - 9t, s, -83 + 17s + 16t, t)$ and $(-10, 49, 0, -83, 0)$.

3. From the system

(2) $\qquad \begin{cases} 2x_1 - 3x_2 + 4x_3 = 0, \\ x_1 + x_2 \qquad = 7, \end{cases}$

of the text, form a new system with the same first equation but with the second equation replaced by its square, $(x_1 + x_2)^2 = 49$. (Do not be concerned about the nonlinearity.) Show that the new system is not equivalent to (2). More specifically, every solution of (2) is a solution of the new system, but not conversely.

4. Let the two systems

(1) $\qquad \begin{cases} a_{11}x_1 + a_{12}x_2 + a_{13}x_3 = b_1, \\ a_{21}x_1 + a_{22}x_2 + a_{23}x_3 = b_2, \end{cases}$

$$(2) \quad \begin{cases} c_{11}x_1 + c_{12}x_2 + c_{13}x_3 = d_1, \\ c_{21}x_1 + c_{22}x_2 + c_{23}x_3 = d_2, \\ c_{31}x_1 + c_{32}x_2 + c_{33}x_3 = d_3, \end{cases}$$

be equivalent. Form two new systems by deleting from each of (1) and (2) all terms containing the variable $x_3$. Prove that the two new systems, in the variables $x_1$ and $x_2$, are also equivalent.

5. Prove that the system

$$(1) \quad \begin{cases} 2x_1 + x_2 - 2x_3 = 17, \\ x_1 \quad\;\;\; - x_3 = 7, \end{cases}$$

is not equivalent to any system in $\{x_1, x_3\}$-basic form.

   *Note:* You cannot rigorously prove this by stating that there is no way to pivot (1) to obtain the basis $\{x_1, x_3\}$. This is not the definition of "not equivalent," nor do we have a theorem to justify this reasoning. You can give a correct proof as follows. Write down a general system with variables $x_1, x_2, x_3$ and basis $\{x_1, x_3\}$. Then specify a solution of this system that is not a solution of (1).

6. Prove there is no system with basis $\{x_2, x_5, x_3\}$ equivalent to the system represented by the tableau below.

|   | 1 | 3 |   |
|---|---|---|---|
| 2 | 3 | −1 | 2 |
| 5 | 2 | 3 | 0 |
| 4 | 1 | 0 | 7 |

7. Consider all possible systems in basic form with three equations and with variables $x_1, \ldots, x_5$. (One such system is that of Problem 6.) Show that there are ten possible choices of bases. In other words, show that the set $\{x_1, \ldots, x_5\}$ has ten subsets with three elements. [A symbol for the number of such subsets is $\binom{5}{3}$.] Next, for a *given* system of the type described, explain why there are *at most* nine other bases obtainable by repeated pivoting, arbitrarily many times. Use Theorem 5 to conclude that there are at most nine other *systems* so obtainable.

8. For the tableau in Problem 6, there are exactly eight other tableaux obtainable by repeated pivoting. Find all of them. (Tableaux differing by only a permutation of the rows or columns, together with headings, are considered identical.)

9. Give your own proof of the pivoting rules of Theorem 6 for the special case indicated below.

|   | 1 | 2 |   |
|---|---|---|---|
| 3 | $(a_{11})$ | $a_{12}$ | $b_1$ |
| 4 | $a_{21}$ | $a_{22}$ | $b_2$ |

$a_{11} \neq 0.$

10. For certain numbers $a$, $b$, $c$, and $d$, the two systems

(1)
$$\begin{cases} x_1 + 5x_2 \quad\;\; = 6, \\ \qquad 7x_2 + x_3 = 8, \end{cases}$$

(2)
$$\begin{cases} x_1 + ax_2 \quad\;\; = b, \\ \qquad cx_2 + x_3 = d, \end{cases}$$

are equivalent. Using the fact that certain specific solutions of (1) must also be solutions of (2), prove that $a = 5$ and $b = 6$. (Do not merely observe that this is a special case of Theorem 5.)

# CHAPTER 2

# Linear Programming Foundations

Linear programming (LP) definitions and other preliminaries are the subjects of this chapter; systematic methods of solving LP problems begin in Chapter 3. The term *programming* here does not refer to computers, although LP problems are widely, frequently, and almost exclusively solved on computers. Rather, the term is a synonym for general *planning* or *scheduling*, as in the phrase "programming of activities." The words *allocating, routing*, and *assigning* often appear in LP problems and, therefore, clarify further the meaning of "programming" in the name of our subject. Some general examples of such programming are the following: allocating time among users of certain equipment, routing long-distance telephone calls through many cities, planning how much fuel an aircraft will take on at various stops, and assigning quantities of crude oil to several refineries. Two important LP problems, known as the *production problem* and the *diet problem*, are formulated in detail in this chapter. All these programming problems, and many others, are of considerable significance to industries such as telecommunications, airlines, petroleum, transportation, and food. In addition, many science, economics, and military problems involve LP. Thus, among mathematical disciplines linear programming is one of extraordinary applicability. The *1988 Book of the Year* of the *Encyclopedia Brittanica* states that hundreds of thousands of LP problems are solved each day! We are content to discuss a few classical problems and some small-scale numerical examples. These problems and examples will convey some of the flavor of applied linear programming and also serve to illustrate the underlying theory. The theory will be our principal concern. For a modern, more advanced treatment of LP, covering many more aspects of the subject, the author recommends Reference [3]. See also [4] by G.B. Dantzig, the principal developer of LP.

An LP problem of great industrial importance is the "production problem." In general form the problem concerns the manufacture of *products* $P_1, \ldots, P_n$

from *resources* $R_1, \ldots, R_m$. (Examples of resources are raw materials, labor, equipment, and time.) There are usually limitations, for example, weekly limitations, on the resources. With appropriate units in mind, we can let $b_i$ $(i = 1, 2, \ldots, m)$ be the amount of resource $R_i$ available to the manufacturer. The manufacturer knows these amounts and knows also how much of each resource is needed in the manufacture of each product. To express the latter, we let $a_{ij}$ be the number of units of $R_i$ required for one unit of $P_j$ $(1 \le i \le m,$ $1 \le j \le n)$. Finally, the net profit resulting from the production of one unit of $P_j$ is known, say $c_j$. The manufacturer would like to determine an optimal production schedule. More explicitly, how much of each product should be made in order that total profits be maximized?

To express the problem precisely, we let $x_j$ be the number of units of $P_j$ to be produced $(1 \le j \le n)$. The $x_j$ must satisfy certain *constraints* or conditions. First, it is clear that we should require each $x_j$ to be nonnegative. The remaining constraints are derived as follows. Since *one* unit of $P_j$ requires $a_{ij}$ units of $R_i$ $(1 \le i \le m)$, a proportionality assumption implies that $x_j$ units of $P_j$ will require $a_{ij}x_j$ units of $R_i$. Therefore, *all* the products will require $\sum_{j=1}^{n} a_{ij}x_j$ units of $R_i$. (We are assuming that the amount of a resource needed for all the products is simply the sum of the amounts needed for each. Other relationships are possible, but this one is by far the most natural and most useful.) For each $i$ the last written sum must be less than or equal to $b_i$. This completes the derivation of the constraints. Finally, from the definitions of $c_j$ and $x_j$ we deduce that $c_j x_j$ is the net profit resulting from the production of $x_j$ units of $P_j$, and hence that $\sum_{j=1}^{n} c_j x_j$ will be the total profit. (Again we are making certain reasonable assumptions.) Thus, the precise statement of the production problem is to

$$\text{maximize} \quad f(x_1, \ldots, x_n) = \sum_{j=1}^{n} c_j x_j \tag{1}$$

subject to the constraints

$$\sum_{j=1}^{n} a_{ij}x_j \le b_i \qquad \text{for all } i, \quad 1 \le i \le m, \tag{2}$$

and the nonnegativity constraints

$$x_j \ge 0, \qquad \text{for all } j, \quad 1 \le j \le n. \tag{3}$$

The phrase "subject to the constraints" means that *the domain of the function f shall consist only of those n-tuples of real numbers obeying all the conditions stated.* The nonnegativity conditions (3) may seem trivial or incidental in the production problem, but such constraints play a crucial role in the solution of LP problems.

The constraints (2) are written very compactly, and it is important to be aware of their expanded form:

$$\begin{aligned}
a_{11}x_1 + a_{12}x_2 + \cdots + a_{1n}x_n &\le b_1, \\
a_{21}x_1 + a_{22}x_2 + \cdots + a_{2n}x_n &\le b_2, \\
\vdots \qquad \vdots \qquad \vdots \qquad \vdots \qquad \vdots \quad & \\
a_{m1}x_1 + a_{m2}x_2 + \cdots + a_{mn}x_n &\le b_m.
\end{aligned} \tag{2}$$

A function of the form in (1) is described as "a linear function of $n$ variables." Likewise, the expressions in (2) are linear. As we shall shortly see, such linearity exists, by definition, for all LP problems. Thus, both words in the term "linear programming" have been explained.

In the production problem just discussed, the quantities $b_i$, $c_j$, and $a_{ij}$ are normally all nonnegative. Except for this fact, the problem defined by (1) through (3) is the most general LP problem in what is called *primal form*. Such problems will prove to be desirable and important. First of all, these are in essence the problems that we shall learn to solve (in Chapters 3 and 4). Second, problems in primal form lie at the foundation of "duality theory" in Chapter 5. The required definition is the following.

**Definition 1.** Given natural numbers $m$ and $n$, and real numbers $b_i$, $c_j$, and $a_{ij}$ $(i = 1, \ldots, m; j = 1, \ldots, n)$, the maximization problem defined by (1) through (3) is an *LP problem in primal form*. The function $f$ in (1), with domain restricted according to the *constraints* (2) and (3), is called the *objective function*.

We shall soon discuss other LP problems, including numerical examples. First, we introduce the *general* LP problem by listing all the permitted deviations from Definition 1. We shall see afterward, however, that the general problem can be reduced to one in primal form with no theoretical loss of generality. As already suggested, this fact will prove to be very useful. The variations of (1), (2), and (3) to be allowed in the general LP problem will be numbered (i), (ii), and (iii), respectively. They are the following.

(i) It may be desired to minimize instead of maximize a linear function, that is, a function of the form in (1). Also, in the course of solving LP problems we shall encounter formulas of the form in (1) plus a constant.

(ii) Instead of $\leq$ inequalities throughout (2), there can be an arbitrary mixture of $\leq$, $\geq$, and $=$ linear relationships. The strict inequalities, $<$ and $>$, are unimportant in applications, as well as troublesome in theory. Consequently, we do not consider them.

(iii) Although the nonnegativity constraints (3) are vital to the theory we shall develop and also generally present in applications, we can temporarily suppose that some or all of these constraints are missing.

Thus we arrive at our second definition.

**Definition 2.** The *general LP problem* is to maximize or minimize (one of these two requirements being specified) a function of the form

$$\sum_{k=1}^{q} c_k x_k + d \tag{4}$$

subject to a finite number of *constraints* of the form

$$\sum_{k=1}^{q} a_k x_k \, (\leq, \geq, =) \, b. \tag{5}$$

In each constraint any one of the three specified relations is permissible, and different constraints can have different relations. The function with formula (4) and with domain restricted by all the constraints (5) is called the *objective function* of the LP problem.

Let us now discuss how we can overcome the deviatons (i) through (iii) from (1) through (3) and thereby return to primal form. Regarding (i), the problem of minimizing any real-valued function is so closely related to that of maximizing its negative that any conclusion concerning the latter problem can immediately be transferred to the original problem. Specifically, let $\varphi$ be any real-valued function on any domain $D$, and suppose it is desired to find the minimum of $\varphi$. Define $\psi = -\varphi$, that is, $\psi(d) = -\varphi(d)$ for every $d \in D$. Suppose $\psi$ attains a maximum at some element $d^*$ of $D$. This means that

$$\psi(d^*) \geq \psi(d), \qquad \text{for all } d \in D.$$

Hence, by definition of $\psi$, $-\varphi(d^*) \geq -\varphi(d)$, and therefore

$$\varphi(d^*) \leq \varphi(d), \qquad \text{for all } d \in D.$$

Thus $\varphi$ achieves a minimum at $d^*$, the same element at which $\psi$ achieves its maximum. In summary,

$$\psi = -\varphi, \qquad \psi(d^*) = \max \psi \quad \Rightarrow \quad \varphi(d^*) = \min \varphi; \qquad (6)$$

and since $\varphi(d^*) = -\psi(d^*)$,

$$\min \varphi = -\max \psi. \qquad (7)$$

Here and elsewhwere the reader should clearly distinguish between the following two questions: What is the minimum or maximum value of a given function? Where (in the domain) does the minimum or maximum occur? The information in (6) and (7) is helpful when we are required to solve certain minimization problems, but we elect to do maximization. We shall shortly illustrate this.

Another possibility for the function $\psi$ is that it is *unbounded above*. [Think of $\psi(x) = x^2$, for example, with domain the set $\mathbf{R}$ of all real numbers.] This means that given any number $M$, no matter how large, there is at least one element $d \in D$ such that $\psi(d) > M$. Since $\psi = -\varphi$, we deduce that $-\varphi(d) > M$ and therefore $\varphi(d) < -M$. Hence $\varphi$ is *unbounded below*; that is, given any number, no matter how small, there is a value of $\varphi$ that is still smaller.

A final possibility is that $\psi$ is *bounded above* but still has no maximum value. For example, suppose the domain $D$ of $\psi$ (and therefore also of $\varphi$) is the set $\mathbf{R}$ of all real numbers, and $\psi(x) = x^2/(x^2 + 1)$. Then $\psi(x) < 1$ for all real $x$, but $\psi(x)$ can come arbitrarily close to 1. It follows that $\psi$ has no maximum value. The corresponding behavior of $\varphi$ is clear: $\varphi$ is *bounded below* but has no minimum. We shall see later that *the behavior described in this paragraph cannot occur in LP*. That is, the function in Definition 2 either has a maximum or is unbounded above, and also either has a minimum or is unbounded below. [Actually, there is also the possibility, to which we shall return, that there are no $q$-tuples of real numbers satisfying all the conditions (5). In other words, the domain of the objective function could be empty.]

It should now be clear precisely how any minimization problem can be replaced by a closely related maximization problem, with easy transfer of any conclusions. The relationship between two functions differing by a constant, the other situation mentioned in (i) above, is less important and also more obvious, so we leave this untreated. In any case, any LP problem can be reduced to one beginning with the description (1) (and any results concerning the modified problem easily applied to the original problem).

Regarding (ii), any $\geq$ inequality in (5) can be converted to $\leq$ by multiplication by $-1$. (We would not wish to do this to an inequality of the form $x_j \geq 0$.) Second, any equality constraint $\sum_{k=1}^{q} a_k x_k = b$ is fully equivalent to the pair of inequalities $\sum_{k=1}^{q} a_k x_k \leq b$ and $\sum_{k=1}^{q} a_k x_k \geq b$. That is, any $q$-tuple of numbers satisfying the given equality satisfies both of the inequalities following, and conversely. The $\geq$ inequality so obtained can then be converted to $\leq$, as already explained. Thus an arbitrary collection (5) can be replaced by an equivalent collection of the form (2). This is the second step that may be needed in reduction to primal form.

We remark that the first step, namely, the replacement of minimization by maximization, changes an LP problem slightly; the change may be measured by (7). However the elimination of $\geq$ and $=$ constraints in the manner described produces a mathematically identical problem. Indeed, neither the formula nor the domain of the objective function is thereby changed. Only the *description* (5) of this domain is altered. We shall see in the next chapter that the simplex algorithm for solving LP problems depends on repeated changes in domain descriptions and also on changes in the manner of computation of the objective function. Mathematically, the problem never changes.

Finally, as for (iii), any variable $x_j$ not constrained to be nonnegative in an LP problem can be replaced by the difference $x_j' - x_j''$ of two nonnegative variables. For the reasons mentioned in (iii) we shall not go into details, and *from now on we shall always assume nonnegativity constraints on all LP variables.*

We now formulate a definition based on our discussion of (i) through (iii).

**Definition 3.** An LP problem in primal form, obtained from another LP problem by one or more of the described techniques for dealing with (i) through (iii), is called the *primal form replacement* of the given problem.

Let us illustrate this definition by means of the following problem.

$$\text{Minimize} \quad g(x_1, x_2, x_3) = 2x_1 + x_2 + 3x_3$$

subject to

$$-3x_1 + 2x_2 + 4x_3 \geq 20,$$
$$x_1 + x_2 + x_3 = 7, \qquad x_1, x_2, x_3 \geq 0.$$

(In practical LP problems, unlike the specific examples in this book, there are often hundreds or even thousands of variables and constraints.) The primal form replacement of this problem is the problem of

$$\text{maximizing} \quad f(x_1, x_2, x_3) = -2x_1 - x_2 - 3x_3$$

subject to

$$3x_1 - 2x_2 - 4x_3 \leq -20,$$

$$x_1 + x_2 + x_3 \leq 7, \qquad x_1, x_2, x_3 \geq 0,$$

$$-x_1 - x_2 - x_3 \leq -7.$$

To illustrate (6) and (7) also, let us suppose that one somehow determines that $\max f = -13$, and that this maximum occurs at $(0, 4, 3)$. (In the problem section of Chapter 4 you will be asked to establish these facts.) Then $\min g = 13$, with this minimum attained at $(0, 4, 3)$.

A classical example of an LP problem not in primal form is the *diet problem*. Suppose nutrients $N_1, \ldots, N_m$ are needed in the daily diet, and certain available foods $F_1, \ldots, F_n$ contain various amounts of these nutrients. Let the following quantities be known.

For $1 \leq i \leq m$, $b_i = $ minimum daily requirement (MDR) of $N_i$ (e.g., in grams).

For $1 \leq j \leq n$, $c_j = $ cost per unit of $F_j$ (e.g., in dollars per gram).

For each such $i$ and $j$, $a_{ij} = $ number of units of $N_i$ contained in each unit of $F_j$.

It is desired to meet the MDRs of all the nutrients as inexpensively as possible. To express this precisely, we let

$$x_j = \text{number of units of } F_j \text{ to be consumed daily.}$$

Then, by definition of $a_{ij}$ and $x_j$,

$$a_{ij}x_j = \text{number of units of } N_i \text{ in the daily ration of } F_j,$$

and therefore

$$\sum_{j=1}^{n} a_{ij}x_j = \text{number of units of } N_i \text{ in the daily diet.}$$

"Meeting the MDRs" then means that

$$\sum_{j=1}^{n} a_{ij}x_j \geq b_i, \qquad \text{for all } i, \quad 1 \leq i \leq m.$$

Next, by definition of $c_j$ and $x_j$,

$$c_j x_j = \text{cost of daily ration of } F_j,$$

and therefore

$$\sum_{j=1}^{n} c_j x_j = \text{total cost of daily diet.}$$

Thus, the mathematical statement of the diet problem is to minimize the previous sum subject to the $\geq$ constraints above and the nonnegativity constraints

$$x_j \geq 0, \quad \text{for all } j, \quad 1 \leq j \leq n.$$

The primal form replacement of the diet problem is the problem of

$$\text{maximizing} \quad f(x_1, \ldots, x_n) = \sum_{j=1}^{n} (-c_j)x_j$$

subject to

$$\sum_{j}^{n} (-a_{ij})x_j \leq -b_i \quad \text{for all } i, \quad 1 \leq i \leq m,$$

and the nonnegativity constraints written above. Numerical examples of both the diet and production problems appear at the end of the chapter.

Returning to the theory, we now require a barrage of definitions supplementing Definition 2. Afterward we illustrate.

**Definition 4.** Given an LP problem with $q$ variables, as in Definition 2, a $q$-tuple of real numbers satisfying all the constraints of the problem is called a *feasible solution*. Any feasible solution at which the objective function attains its required maximum or minimum is called an *optimal feasible solution* (OFS). An LP problem with no feasible solution is called an *infeasible problem*; otherwise, a *feasible problem*. The set of all feasible solutions is the *feasible region*.

A couple of comments may be helpful. First, a feasible solution is only a "solution of the system of constraints," not a "solution of the LP problem." Concerning the latter phrase, the concept of OFS and Definition 5 below are relevant. Second, we observe that by Definitions 2 and 4 *the feasible region of an LP problem is the domain of the objective function*.

Definition 4 indicates two of the possible outcomes of an LP problem, namely, the determination of an OFS or the determination that the problem is infeasible. A third possibility is that the objective function is "unbounded in the relevant direction." (Unbounded above if the problem requires maximization, unbounded below for minimization.) As mentioned earlier, it is impossible for an objective function in a feasible LP problem to be bounded above (respectively, below) and not achieve a maximum (respectively, a minimum). Anticipating the establishing of this result, we put forth the following definition.

**Definition 5.** *Solving an LP problem* means either

(a) finding an OFS and the corresponding value of the objective function, or
(b) showing that the objective function is unbounded in the relevant direction, or
(c) showing that the problem is infeasible.

We repeat for emphasis, especially with regard to (b), that the objective function is to be evaluated only at feasible solutions. It should then be clear that outcomes (a), (b), and (c) are mutually exclusive.

Let us now illustrate outcome (a) and, at the same time, some notions in Definition 4. We consider the problem (in primal form) of

$$\text{maximizing} \quad f(x_1, x_2) = -2x_1 + 7x_2$$

subject to

$$x_1 + x_2 \leq 5,$$
$$3x_2 \leq 2, \qquad x_1, x_2 \geq 0.$$

The problem can be solved by the following ad hoc method. First, we note that feasible solutions exist, for example, $(0, 0)$. Next, for *any* feasible solution $(s_1, s_2)$,

$$f(s_1, s_2) = -2s_1 + 7s_2 \leq 7s_2 \leq \tfrac{14}{3}.$$

The first inequality holds because $s_1 \geq 0$; the second, because $s_2 \leq \tfrac{2}{3}$. This computation shows that $\tfrac{14}{3}$ is an upper bound for $f$. The computation also shows that $f(s_1, s_2) = \tfrac{14}{3}$ if and only if $s_1 = 0$ and $s_2 = \tfrac{2}{3}$. It is then easy to check that $(0, \tfrac{2}{3})$ is a feasible solution. Hence $\max f = \tfrac{14}{3}$ and $(0, \tfrac{2}{3})$ is an OFS. Figure 1 shows the feasible region and the OFS $(0, \tfrac{2}{3})$.

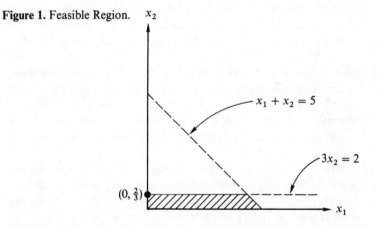

**Figure 1.** Feasible Region.

We note that if the constraint $3x_2 \leq 2$ were replaced by the strict inequality $3x_2 < 2$ (not permitted in LP), the objective function would be bounded above by $\tfrac{14}{3}$ but would not have a maximum value. The verification is left to the interested reader, if any.

In the original problem there is only one OFS, but the situation is quite different if the objective function is changed to $7x_1 + 7x_2$, for example. All ordered pairs $(s_1, s_2)$ satisfying $s_1 + s_2 = 5$ and $0 \leq s_2 \leq \tfrac{2}{3}$ are then OFSs. (Details?) *In any case, at least one vertex of the feasible region is an OFS if OFSs exist.* See Problem 4.

An example of outcome (b) of Definition 5 results from the problem of

$$\text{maximizing} \quad f(x_1, x_2) = -2x_1 + 7x_2$$

subject to

$$-2x_1 + x_2 \leq 3,$$
$$x_1 - x_2 \leq 1,$$
$$x_1, x_2 \geq 0.$$

For this problem it is easy to check that $(t, t)$ is a feasible solution for every $t \geq 0$, while $f(t, t) = 5t$. Thus it is clear that $f$ is unbounded above.

Finally, to illustrate (c), let us suppose that the constraints of an LP problem are the following:

$$2x_1 - 3x_2 \leq -4,$$
$$x_1 + x_2 \leq 1,$$
$$x_1, x_2 \geq 0.$$

If a feasible solution $(s_1, s_2)$ existed, there would follow

$$2s_1 - 3s_2 \leq -4,$$
$$3s_1 + 3s_2 \leq 3,$$
$$\text{(adding)} \quad 5s_1 \leq -1,$$

contradicting the nonnegativity of $s_1$. Hence such a problem is infeasible.

We have employed ad hoc approaches to solve the last three illustrative problems, but later we shall have more systematic, mechanical methods.

The final topic of Chapter 2 is the association with each primal form LP problem of an *enlarged* LP problem, in which additional variables are present. More explicitly, each $\leq$ constraint of the primal problem is replaced by an equality constraint with a new nonnegative variable added to the left side. Such enlarged problems are of great utility in LP because, roughly speaking, equations are easier to handle than inequalities. (The exact details will have to wait for Chapters 3 and 4.) Once the enlarged problem is solved, conclusions are immediately transferable to the problem in primal form from which it arose.

The idea behind *enlargement* is extremely simple: For two numbers, $a$ and $b$, $a \leq b$ if and only if there exists a nonnegative number $c$ such that $a + c = b$. Let us apply this idea to a previously analyzed problem, which we now designate by $\mathscr{P}$. The problem is the following:

$$\mathscr{P}: \quad \begin{cases} \text{Maximize} \quad f(x_1, x_2) = -2x_1 + 7x_2 \\ \text{subject to} \quad x_1 + x_2 \leq 5, \\ \qquad\qquad\qquad 3x_2 \leq 2, \end{cases} \quad x_1, x_2 \geq 0.$$

In accordance with the thought above, we replace the first two constraints by the equality constraints

$$x_1 + x_2 + x_3 = 5,$$
$$3x_2 + x_4 = 2.$$

Here $x_3$ and $x_4$ are new variables, constrained to be nonnegative and called *slack variables*. (Each "takes up the slack" between a "small quantity" and a "large quantity.") The original variables, $x_1$ and $x_2$, are then distinguished by the term *decision variables*. (In practical problems, choosing the values of the decision variables corresponds to making programming decisions.) We note in passing that the new system of equality constraints is in basic form, as defined in Chapter 1, with the slack variables forming a basis. This general circumstance will be extremely useful in future chapters.

For mathematical precision we must now make a change in the objective function. Now that four variables are present, the domain of the objective function will consist of all *4-tuples* that

 (i) are solutions of the previous linear system, and
(ii) have all nonnegative components.

We denote the new objective function by $F$, and write

$$F(x_1, x_2, x_3, x_4) = -2x_1 + 7x_2 + 0x_3 + 0x_4.$$

Again, $F$ is a function of four variables (has domain contained in $\mathbf{R}^4$) even though only $x_1$ and $x_2$ appear on the right side of this formula.

The formula just written for $F$ is not the only one. For instance, by the equality constraint $x_1 + x_2 + x_3 = 5$, we can write

$$F(x_1, x_2, x_3, x_4) = -2(5 - x_2 - x_3) + 7x_2 = -10 + 9x_2 + 2x_3.$$

The underlying logic here is that any 4-tuple $(s_1, s_2, s_3, s_4)$ in the domain of $F$ satisfies all the constraints specified by (i) and (ii) above. In particular, $s_1 + s_2 + s_3 = 5$. Therefore $F(s_1, s_2, s_3, s_4) = -10 + 9s_2 + 2s_3$ by the same computation as that just performed. As mentioned before, we shall later exploit such changes in objective function formulas. Incidentally, the function $f$, unlike $F$, has only one possible formula. This is made precise in Problem 6 at the end of the chapter.

Let us now collect all the pieces of the LP problem we have created out of problem $\mathscr{P}$. The new problem will be called the *enlarged problem* or the *enlargement of problem $\mathscr{P}$*, and will be denoted by $\mathscr{E}(\mathscr{P})$. It is the following.

$$\mathscr{E}(\mathscr{P}): \begin{cases} \text{Maximize} \quad F(x_1, x_2, x_3, x_4) = -2x_1 + 7x_2 \\ \text{subject to} \quad x_1 + x_2 + x_3 = 5, \\ \qquad\qquad\qquad 3x_2 + x_4 = 2, \end{cases} \quad x_1, x_2, x_3, x_4 \geq 0.$$

Problems of the form $\mathscr{E}(\mathscr{P})$, obtainable from LP problems in primal form by adding slack variables, are routinely solved in Chapters 3 and 4. Therefore our immediate question is the following: Given a problem in primal form, how are conclusions concerning the enlarged problem transferred to the given problem? We shall find that the transfer is quite simple and automatic. We illustrate this with the current example; afterward we generalize.

Let us determine the exact relationships between the feasible regions and the objective functions of the problems $\mathscr{P}$ and $\mathscr{E}(\mathscr{P})$ defined above. It will be convenient to denote the respective feasible regions by $\mathscr{R}$ and $\mathscr{E}(\mathscr{R})$. Specifically,

$$\mathscr{R} = \{(s_1, s_2) \,|\, s_1 + s_2 \leq 5; \; 3s_2 \leq 2; \; s_1, s_2 \geq 0\},$$

$$\mathscr{E}(\mathscr{R}) = \{(s_1, s_2, s_3, s_4) \,|\, s_1 + s_2 + s_3 = 5; \; 3s_2 + s_4 = 2;$$

$$s_1, s_2, s_3, s_4 \geq 0\}.$$

We show that $\mathscr{R}$ and $\mathscr{E}(\mathscr{R})$ are in one-to-one correspondence. First, let $(s_1, s_2, s_3, s_4) \in \mathscr{E}(\mathscr{R})$. Since $s_1 + s_2 + s_3 = 5$, while $s_3 \geq 0$, it is clear that $s_1 + s_2 \leq 5$. Similarly, $3s_2 \leq 2$. Since $s_1$ and $s_2$ are also nonnegative, we conclude that $(s_1, s_2) \in \mathscr{R}$. Thus, we can "go from $\mathscr{E}(\mathscr{R})$ to $\mathscr{R}$" by the simple procedure of dropping the last two components.

Conversely, suppose $(s_1, s_2)$ is an arbitrary element of $\mathscr{R}$. We assert that there are unique numbers $s_3$ and $s_4$ such that the 4-tuple $(s_1, s_2, s_3, s_4)$ belongs to $\mathscr{E}(\mathscr{R})$. Indeed, there is one and only one number $s_3$ such that $s_1 + s_2 + s_3 = 5$ (namely, $5 - s_1 - s_2$). Furthermore, since $s_1 + s_2 \leq 5$, it is clear that $s_3 \geq 0$. A similar analysis holds for $s_4$, the desired fourth component. Thus, $(s_1, s_2, s_3, s_4) \in \mathscr{E}(\mathscr{R})$, and for no other 4-tuple with $s_1$ and $s_2$ as the first two components is this statement true. We have thus demonstrated a one-to-one correspondence between $\mathscr{R}$ and $\mathscr{E}(\mathscr{R})$, as promised.

We can now bring the objective functions $f$ and $F$ into the discussion. The domains of these functions, we recall, are precisely $\mathscr{R}$ and $\mathscr{E}(\mathscr{R})$, respectively. If $(s_1, s_2)$ and $(s_1, s_2, s_3, s_4)$ are any two corresponding elements of these respective domains, the definitions of $f$ and $F$ give $f(s_1, s_2) = -2s_1 + 7s_2 = F(s_1, s_2, s_3, s_4)$. In words, $f$ and $F$ agree at corresponding elements of $\mathscr{R}$ and $\mathscr{E}(\mathscr{R})$, respectively. It follows easily from this that $(s_1, s_2)$ is an OFS of problem $\mathscr{P}$ if and only if $(s_1, s_2, s_3, s_4)$ is an OFS of $\mathscr{E}(\mathscr{P})$. To illustrate, we recall that $(0, \frac{2}{3})$ is an OFS of $\mathscr{P}$. The corresponding element of $\mathscr{E}(\mathscr{R})$, determined from the equality constraints of $\mathscr{E}(\mathscr{P})$, is $(0, \frac{2}{3}, \frac{13}{3}, 0)$. The assertion that this 4-tuple is an OFS of $\mathscr{E}(\mathscr{P})$ means that

$$F(0, \tfrac{2}{3}, \tfrac{13}{3}, 0) \geq F(t_1, t_2, t_3, t_4)$$

for every element $(t_1, t_2, t_3, t_4)$ of $\mathscr{E}(\mathscr{R})$. But for any such element, we know that $(t_1, t_2) \in \mathscr{R}$, and that the asserted inequality is exactly the same as

$$f(0, \tfrac{2}{3}) \geq f(t_1, t_2).$$

This inequality, of course, is true because $(0, \frac{2}{3})$ is an OFS of $\mathscr{P}$.

It is normal in linear programming to find an OFS of the enlarged problem first. If we had known first that $(0, \frac{2}{3}, \frac{13}{3}, 0)$ was an OFS of $\mathscr{E}(\mathscr{P})$, we could have reasoned as follows: An arbitrary element $(t_1, t_2)$ of $\mathscr{R}$ can be "extended" to an element $(t_1, t_2, t_3, t_4)$ of $\mathscr{E}(\mathscr{R})$. Then $F(0, \frac{2}{3}, \frac{13}{3}, 0) \geq F(t_1, t_2, t_3, t_4)$. Therefore $f(0, \frac{2}{3}) \geq f(t_1, t_2)$, as required to demonstrate that $(0, \frac{2}{3})$ is an OFS of $\mathscr{P}$. In summary: *Given an OFS of $\mathscr{E}(\mathscr{P})$, simply discard the slack variable components to obtain an OFS of $\mathscr{P}$.*

We conclude the chapter by generalizing our discussion of $\mathscr{P}$ and $\mathscr{E}(\mathscr{P})$.

**Definition 6.** Given the LP problem in primal form defined by (1) through (3), the *enlarged problem* is to

maximize $\quad F(x_1, \ldots, x_n, x_{n+1}, \ldots, x_{n+m})$

$$= c_1 x_1 + \cdots + c_n x_n + 0 x_{n+1} + \cdots + 0 x_{n+m} \quad (1')$$

subject to the constraints

$$\sum_{j=1}^{n} a_{ij} x_j + x_{n+i} = b_i, \qquad \text{for all } i, \quad 1 \le i \le m \quad (2')$$

and

$$x_k \ge 0, \qquad \text{for all } k, \quad 1 \le k \le n + m. \quad (3')$$

The variables $x_{n+1}, \ldots, x_{n+m}$ are called *slack variables*; the variables $x_1, \ldots, x_n$, *decision variables*.

The import of our final theorem is that any problem in primal form has the same outcome as its enlargement.

**Theorem 1.** *Let $\mathcal{P}$ be the primal form LP problem (1) through (3), and let $\mathcal{E}(\mathcal{P})$ be the corresponding enlarged problem (1') through (3'). Let $\mathcal{R}$ be the feasible region of problem $\mathcal{P}$, and let $\mathcal{E}(\mathcal{R})$ be the feasible region of problem $\mathcal{E}(\mathcal{P})$. The following assertions then hold.*

(i)  *The mapping $(s_1, \ldots, s_n, s_{n+1}, \ldots, s_{n+m}) \to (s_1, \ldots, s_n)$, discarding the last $m$ components, provides a one-to-one correspondence of $\mathcal{E}(\mathcal{R})$ onto $\mathcal{R}$.*
(ii)  *If $(s_1, \ldots, s_n, s_{n+1}, \ldots, s_{n+m}) \in \mathcal{E}(\mathcal{R})$, then*

$$F(s_1, \ldots, s_n, s_{n+1}, \ldots, s_{n+m}) = f(s_1, \ldots, s_n);$$

   *that is, $F$ and $f$ agree at corresponding elements of their respective domains.*
(iii)  *The $(n + m)$-tuple $(s_1^*, \ldots, s_n^*, s_{n+1}^*, \ldots, s_{n+m}^*)$ is an OFS of $\mathcal{E}(\mathcal{P})$ if and only if $(s_1^*, \ldots, s_n^*)$ is an OFS of $\mathcal{P}$, and then $\max F = \max f$.*
(iv)  *$F$ is unbounded above [on $\mathcal{E}(\mathcal{R})$] if and only if $f$ is unbounded above [on $\mathcal{R}$.]*
(v)  *$\mathcal{P}$ is infeasible if and only if $\mathcal{E}(\mathcal{P})$ is infeasible.*

*Proof.* We first show that $(s_1, \ldots, s_{n+m}) \in \mathcal{E}(\mathcal{R})$ implies $(s_1, \ldots, s_n) \in \mathcal{R}$. If $(s_1, \ldots, s_{n+m}) \in \mathcal{E}(\mathcal{R})$, then (2') and (3') are satisfied; that is,

$$\sum_{j=1}^{n} a_{ij} s_j + s_{n+i} = b_i, \qquad 1 \le i \le m,$$

and

$$s_k \ge 0, \qquad 1 \le k \le n + m.$$

Therefore

$$\sum_{j=1}^{n} a_{ij} s_j \le b_i, \qquad 1 \le i \le m,$$

and $(s_1, \ldots, s_n)$ satisfies (2). Clearly $(s_1, \ldots, s_n)$ satisfies (3). Hence $(s_1, \ldots, s_n) \in \mathscr{R}$, as asserted.

To complete the proof of (i), we let $(s_1, \ldots, s_n)$ be an arbitrary element of $\mathscr{R}$ and show that there are uniquely determined numbers $s_{n+1}, \ldots, s_{n+m}$ such that $(s_1, \ldots, s_n, s_{n+1}, \ldots, s_{n+m}) \in \mathscr{E}(\mathscr{R})$. Indeed, since

$$\sum_{j=1}^{n} a_{ij}s_j \leq b_i, \qquad 1 \leq i \leq m,$$

we can define

$$s_{n+i} = b_i - \sum_{j=1}^{n} a_{ij}s_j, \qquad 1 \leq i \leq m,$$

and have $s_{n+i} \geq 0$, as required for (3'). Moreover, it is clear that these choices of $s_{n+i}$ $(1 \leq i \leq m)$ are the only choices satisfying (2'). Thus $(s_1, \ldots, s_n, s_{n+1}, \ldots, s_{n+m}) \in \mathscr{E}(\mathscr{R})$, and for no other choice of the last $m$ components is this statement true. Assertion (i) is now proved.

Assertion (ii) now follows from the definitions of $f$ and $F$. For conclusions (iii) we use (i) and (ii) to deduce that an $(n + m)$-tuple $(s_1^*, \ldots, s_n^*, s_{n+1}^*, \ldots, s_{n+m}^*)$ belonging to $\mathscr{E}(\mathscr{R})$ satisfies

$$F(s_1^*, \ldots, s_n^*, s_{n+1}^*, \ldots, s_{n+m}^*) \geq F(s_1, \ldots, s_n, s_{n+1}, \ldots, s_{n+m})$$

for all $(s_1, \ldots, s_n, s_{n+1}, \ldots, s_{n+m}) \in \mathscr{E}(\mathscr{R})$ if and only if

$$f(s_1^*, \ldots, s_n^*) \geq f(s_1, \ldots, s_n)$$

for all $(s_1, \ldots, s_n) \in \mathscr{R}$.

Finally, (iv) follows directly from (i) and (ii), and (v) is an immediate consequence of (i). [$\mathscr{R}$ is empty if and only if $\mathscr{E}(\mathscr{R})$ is empty.]    $\square$

In the next two chapters we shall learn to solve LP problems of the form (1') through (3'). Chapter 3 deals mostly with the case in which $b_i \geq 0$ (for all $i$, $1 \leq i \leq m$); Chapter 4 treats the remaining situation. The computational tool for solving all such problems will be the pivoting of condensed tableaux.

## PROBLEMS

1. Express the boat production problem described below as an LP problem in primal form. In doing so, do not be concerned about the following facts.
   (i) The given data on boat building are not genuine.
   (ii) Optimal feasible solutions of LP problems are likely to contain one or more noninteger components, even if only integers appear in the given data. In the problem below, this would mean building fractional numbers of boats. Assuming this makes no sense, we would then have to turn for guidance to the subject called *integer programming*. Actually, the problem about to be described turns out to be free of such difficulties. At the end of Chapter 3 you will be asked to solve the problem completely. There will be a unique OFS, and it will have all integer components.

Here is the problem: A manufacturer builds three types of boats: rowboats, canoes, and kayaks. They sell at profits of $200, $150, and $120, respectively, per boat. The boats require aluminum in their construction, and also labor in two sections of the workshop. The following table specifies all the material and labor requirements:

|  | 1 row boat | 1 canoe | 1 kayak |
|---|---|---|---|
| Aluminum | 30 pounds | 15 pounds | 10 pounds |
| Section 1 | 2 hours | 3 hours | 2 hours |
| Section 2 | 1 hour | 1 hour | 1 hour |

The manufacturer can obtain 630 pounds of aluminum in the coming month. Sections 1 and 2 of the workshop have, respectively, 110 and 50 hours available for the month. What monthly production schedule will maximize total profits, and what is the largest possible profit? (Again, *solve* this problem after Chapter 3.)

2. Express the following diet problem in symbols.

   A farmer can buy two animal feeds, $F_1$ and $F_2$. These feeds contain nutrients $N_1$, $N_2$, $N_3$ needed by the farm animals. The chart below states the nutritional content and cost of each feed, and also the MDR (minimum daily requirement) of each nutrient per farm animal.

|  | $F_1$ | $F_2$ | MDR |
|---|---|---|---|
| $N_1$ | 5 | 1 | 11 |
| $N_2$ | 2 | 1 | 8 |
| $N_3$ | 1 | 2 | 7 |
| Cents/pound | 40 | 30 | |

For instance, each pound of $F_1$ contains 5 units of $N_1$, and costs 40 cents; and each animal requires at least 11 units of $N_1$ per day. How can the MDRs be met with minimum cost?

3. On an $x_1$, $x_2$ coordinate system, graph the feasible region $\mathcal{S}$ specified by the following constraints:

$$5x_1 + x_2 \geq 11,$$

$$2x_1 + x_2 \geq 8, \qquad x_1, x_2 \geq 0.$$

$$x_1 + 2x_2 \geq 7,$$

If your work is correct you will find that $\mathcal{S}$ is an unbounded region in the first quadrant, with the boundary consisting of segments of the two coordinate axes and segments of the three lines $5x_1 + x_2 = 11$, $2x_1 + x_2 = 8$, and $x_1 + 2x_2 = 7$. The segments come together and form vertices of $\mathcal{S}$ at $(0, 11)$, $(1, 6)$, $(3, 2)$, and $(7, 0)$.

4. Minimize the function $g(x_1, x_2) = 40x_1 + 30x_2$, subject to the constraints of the last problem. Use the following procedure: Graph the line $40x_1 + 30x_2 = c$ for a

few different values of $c$, say $c = 160$ and $c = 200$. (Such lines can be called *level sets* of $g$. The reason for this name emerges if we temporarily consider the domain of $g$ to be all points in the $x_1$, $x_2$ plane. Then $g$ has the same value, namely, $c$, at every point of such a line.) Among all such lines *that intersect $\mathscr{S}$*, you must find the one for which $c$ is a minimum. Observe that a vertex of $\mathscr{S}$ must inevitably be involved.

*Answer:* min $g = g(3, 2) = 180$.

Diet problem interpretation: Feed each animal 3 pounds of $F_1$ and 2 pounds of $F_2$; the cost is $1.80.

5. Find the enlargement of the primal form replacement of the LP problem considered in Problems 3 and 4. Use your conclusions concerning Problem 4 to solve (Definition 5) this enlarged problem.

*Answer:* max $F = F(3, 2, 6, 0, 0) = -180$.

6. Consider again the problem $\mathscr{P}$ with objective function $f(x_1, x_2) = -2x_1 + 7x_2$, and with feasible region $\mathscr{R}$ as in Figure 1. Show that in the following sense there is no other formula for $f$: If numbers $c_1, c_2,$ and $d$ exist such that $f(s_1, s_2) = c_1 s_1 + c_2 s_2 + d$ for every ordered pair $(s_1, s_2)$ belonging to $\mathscr{R}$, then $c_1 = -2, c_2 = 7,$ and $d = 0$.

*Hint:* Apply the assumption that $-2s_1 + 7s_2 = c_1 s_1 + c_2 s_2 + d$ to some specific pairs.

7. For the same problem $\mathscr{P}$, the system of equality constraints of $\mathscr{E}(\mathscr{P})$ is represented by the following condensed tableau:

$$
\begin{array}{c|cc|c}
 & 1 & 2 & \\
\hline
3 & 1 & 1 & 5 \\
4 & 0 & 3 & 2 \\
\end{array}
$$

For this system and equivalent systems in basic form, there are six conceivable choices of bases. Actually only five such bases are possible, and therefore (Chapter 1, Theorem 5) only five such equivalent systems exist.

(a) Find the four other systems.
(b) Write down all five possible basic solutions [such as $(0, 0, 5, 2)$].
(c) Note that four of these basic solutions have all nonnegative components. Equivalently, four of these basic solutions are feasible solutions of $\mathscr{E}(\mathscr{P})$. Let us call them *feasible basic solutions.*
(d) Discard the slack variable components (third and fourth components) of each feasible basic solution. Observe that the ordered pairs remaining are precisely the four vertices $(0, 0), (0, \frac{2}{3}), (\frac{13}{3}, \frac{2}{3}), (5, 0)$ of $\mathscr{R}$.

It is an interesting fact that the result of this example generalizes. Indeed, "vertex" can be rigorously defined in any number of dimensions, and for *arbitrary* $\mathscr{P}$ and $\mathscr{E}(\mathscr{P})$ (as in Definitions 1 and 6) the following three statements are equivalent:

(i) $(s_1, \ldots, s_{n+m})$ is a feasible basic solution of $\mathscr{E}(\mathscr{P})$.
(ii) $(s_1, \ldots, s_n)$ is a vertex of $\mathscr{R}$.
(iii) $(s_1, \ldots, s_{n+m})$ is a vertex of $\mathscr{E}(\mathscr{R})$.

8. Consider the following LP problem:

$$\text{Maximize} \quad f(x_1, x_2, x_3) = 4x_1 - 3x_2$$
subject to the constraints

$$2x_2 - 3x_3 \leq -1,$$
$$5x_1 \qquad + x_3 \leq \quad 2, \qquad x_1, x_2, x_3 \geq 0.$$

There is a variable that (like a slack variable) "appears" in the constraints but not in the objective function. This should not be considered strange; it is just a matter of a zero coefficient in the objective function. Solving such a problem (by the methods of Chapters 3 and 4) requires no special procedure. Just as an exercise, however, eliminate $x_3$ from the problem. You should obtain the following problem:

$$\text{Maximize} \quad \tilde{f}(x_1, x_2) = 4x_1 - 3x_2$$
subject to the constraints

$$15x_1 + 2x_2 \leq 5, \qquad x_1, x_2, \geq 0.$$

To describe the exact relationship between the first and second problems, let $Q$ and $\tilde{Q}$ be the respective feasible regions. Show that the following three statements hold.

(i) If $(s_1, s_2, s_3) \in Q$, then $(s_1, s_2) \in \tilde{Q}$.
(ii) If $(s_1, s_2) \in \tilde{Q}$, there exists $s_3$ (not necessarily unique) such that $(s_1, s_2, s_3) \in Q$.
(iii) If $s_1, s_2, s_3$ are as in (i) or (ii), then $f(s_1, s_2, s_3) = \tilde{f}(s_1, s_2)$.

Think about how you would use the results of solving either problem to solve the other.

*Hint for* (ii): Given $(s_1, s_2) \in \tilde{Q}$, prove the existence of 2 (nonnegative) number $s_3$ satisfying

$$\tfrac{1}{3}(2s_2 + 1) \leq s_3 \leq 2 - 5s_1.$$

# CHAPTER 3

# The Simplex Algorithm

An *algorithm* is (roughly) a computational procedure or a sequence of instructions for solving a mathematical problem. The simplex algorithm, which we henceforth designate by SIMPLEX, is a pivoting algorithm for solving LP problems of a certain type. The procedure was invented by George B. Dantzig in 1947 and has since been extremely and increasingly useful. Indeed, virtually all practical LP problems are solved by SIMPLEX or some variation thereof. The main purposes of this chapter are to define the type of problem to which SIMPLEX is directly applicable, to set forth the steps of the algorithm, and to explain the underlying theory.

We begin by explaining how *condensed tableaux* can be used to represent certain LP problems. These tableaux are the condensed tableaux of Chapter 1 for systems of simultaneous equations in basic form, but augmented by an additional row for the objective function. To illustrate, we employ the tableau

$$
\begin{array}{c|cccc|c}
 & 1 & 2 & \cdots & n & \\
\hline
n+1 & a_{11} & a_{12} & \cdots & a_{1n} & b_1 \\
n+2 & a_{21} & a_{22} & \cdots & a_{2n} & b_2 \\
\vdots & \vdots & \vdots & & \vdots & \vdots \\
n+m & a_{m1} & a_{m2} & \cdots & a_{mn} & b_m \\
\hline
F & -c_1 & -c_2 & \cdots & -c_n & 0
\end{array}
\tag{1}
$$

to represent the LP problem of maximizing

$$F(x_1, \ldots, x_n, x_{n+1}, \ldots, x_{n+m}) = c_1 x_1 + c_2 x_2 + \cdots + c_n x_n$$

subject to the usual nonnegativity constraints on all $n + m$ variables, and to the equality constraints represented by the top portion of the tableau, namely,

$$x_{n+1} + a_{11}x_1 + a_{12}x_2 + \cdots + a_{1n}x_n = b_1,$$
$$x_{n+2} + a_{21}x_1 + a_{22}x_2 + \cdots + a_{2n}x_n = b_2,$$
$$\vdots \qquad \vdots \qquad \vdots \qquad \vdots \qquad \vdots \qquad \vdots$$
$$x_{n+m} + a_{m1}x_1 + a_{m2}x_2 + \cdots + a_{mn}x_n = b_m.$$

[This LP problem is exactly the enlarged problem (1′), (2′), and (3′) of Chapter 2.]

To construct tableau (1) we have added a row, the *objective row*, to the condensed tableau representation of the linear system just written. The left edge of the tableau, which functions as a plus sign for every equation of the system, now does so also for the objective row. Similarly, the vertical line separating the coefficients from the constants extends down and serves as an equal sign for the objective row. Thus this row reads

$$F - c_1x_1 - c_2x_2 - \cdots - c_nx_n = 0,$$

in agreement with the formula given above. The symbol $F$ here is an abbreviation for $F(x_1, \ldots, x_{n+m})$, but since the variables $x_{n+1}, \ldots, x_{n+m}$ do not appear in the formula for $F$, we have been able to insert all the necessary information into the objective row. We shall shortly need tableaux slightly more general than (1), but in any case, a condensed tableau with an objective row can accommodate an objective function only if the latter is expressed solely in terms of the nonbasic variables of the linear system.

Tableau (1) contains all the information of the LP problem it represents with two exceptions: the explicit requirement that $F$ is to be maximized and an explicit statement of the nonnegativity constraints on $x_1, \ldots, x_{n+m}$. These two requirements are therefore to be tacitly understood from tableaux such as (1). We restate this "understanding" formally in Definition 1 below.

We alluded above to tableaux more general than (1). These come about because we shall have to pivot tableaux of type (1). This pivoting will be as described in Chapter 1 for tableaux like the top portion of (1), but will henceforth include an objective row. As a result of the pivoting, two features not present in tableau (1) will normally appear: row and column headings not in natural order, and nonzero numbers in the lower right corner. Therefore we put forth the following definition.

**Definition 1.** Let $\{j_1, \ldots, j_m, k_1, \ldots, k_n\} = \{1, 2, \ldots, n + m\}$; that is, $j_1, \ldots, j_m$, $k_1, \ldots, k_n$ are the natural numbers $1, 2, \ldots, n + m$ in some order. Then the tableau

|       | $k_1$       | $\cdots$ | $k_n$       |            |
|-------|-------------|----------|-------------|------------|
| $j_1$ | $\alpha_{11}$ | $\cdots$ | $\alpha_{1n}$ | $\beta_1$    |
| $\vdots$ | $\vdots$  |          | $\vdots$    | $\vdots$   |
| $j_m$ | $\alpha_{m1}$ | $\cdots$ | $\alpha_{mn}$ | $\beta_m$    |
| $F$   | $\gamma_1$  | $\cdots$ | $\gamma_n$  | $\delta$   |

(2)

represents the LP problem of maximizing the function $F$ defined by

$$F(x_1, \ldots, x_{n+m}) + \gamma_1 x_{k_1} + \cdots + \gamma_n x_{k_n} = \delta,$$

with constraints

$$\begin{cases} x_{j_1} + \alpha_{11} x_{k_1} + \cdots + \alpha_{1n} x_{k_n} = \beta_1, \\ \vdots \qquad \vdots \qquad \vdots \qquad \vdots \qquad \vdots \\ x_{j_m} + \alpha_{m1} x_{k_1} + \cdots + \alpha_{mn} x_{k_n} = \beta_m, \end{cases}$$

and

$$x_1, x_2, \ldots, x_{n+m} \geq 0.$$

(The $\alpha$'s, $\beta$'s, $\gamma$'s and $\delta$ are given real numbers.) The numbers $\gamma_1, \ldots, \gamma_n$ (but not $\delta$) are called the *objective entries*, and $\delta$, the *corner number* of the tableau.

It is important in connection with SIMPLEX to remember two facts about the objective entries. The first is that the corner number is not included; the second is that the objective entries are the respective *negatives* of the coefficients of the objective function.

Let us consider as an example the problem, discussed in Chapter 2, of maximizing

$$F(x_1, x_2, x_3, x_4) = -2x_1 + 7x_2 + 0x_3 + 0x_4$$

subject to the constraints

$$\begin{cases} x_1 + x_2 + x_3 \qquad = 5, \\ 3x_2 \qquad + x_4 = 2, \end{cases}$$

and $x_1, x_2, x_3, x_4 \geq 0$. A condensed tableau representing this LP problem is

|   | 1 | 2 |   |
|---|---|---|---|
| 3 | 1 | 1 | 5 |
| 4 | 0 | ③ | 2 |
| F | 2 | −7 | 0 |

.

The coefficients $-2$ and $7$ in the formula for $F$ have led to the objective entries $2$ and $-7$.

If we now pivot at 3, as indicated by the circle (and as will be required by SIMPLEX), there results the tableau

|   | 1 | 4 |   |
|---|---|---|---|
| 3 | 1 | $-\frac{1}{3}$ | $\frac{13}{3}$ |
| 2 | 0 | $\frac{1}{3}$ | $\frac{2}{3}$ |
| F | 2 | $\frac{7}{3}$ | $\frac{14}{3}$ |

.

In constructing this tableau we have extended, without justification, the pivoting rules of Chapter 1 (specifically rules 3 and 4 of Theorem 6) to the objective row. This extension seems completely reasonable if we think of the objective row as just another equation, with $F$ as just another basic variable. The precise sense in which the new formula for $F$ is correct and in which *the new tableau represents the same LP problem as the first tableau* is explained as follows. By Definition 1 the last written tableau represents the problem of maximizing

$$F(x_1, x_2, x_3, x_4) = \tfrac{14}{3} - 2x_1 - \tfrac{7}{3}x_4$$

subject to

$$\begin{cases} x_3 + x_1 - \tfrac{1}{3}x_4 = \tfrac{13}{3}, \\ x_2 \qquad + \tfrac{1}{3}x_4 = \tfrac{2}{3}, \end{cases}$$

and $x_1, x_2, x_3, x_4 \geq 0$. We know from Chapter 1 that this linear system is equivalent to the preceding one. Consequently, our two LP problems have the same feasible solutions. In other words, the two objective functions have the same domain.

As for the two objective function formulas, we have the computation

$$-2x_1 + 7x_2 = -2x_1 + 7(\tfrac{2}{3} - \tfrac{1}{3}x_4) = \tfrac{14}{3} - 2x_1 - \tfrac{7}{3}x_4.$$

To give a complete logical argument, as in a similar situation in Chapter 2, we need only let $(s_1, s_2, s_3, s_4)$ be an arbitrary element of the domain of $F$. Then $(s_1, s_2, s_3, s_4)$ obeys all the constraints of either of the two tableaux; in particular, $s_2 + \tfrac{1}{3}s_4 = \tfrac{2}{3}$. Therefore $F(s_1, s_2, s_3, s_4) = -2s_1 + 7s_2 = \tfrac{14}{3} - 2s_1 - \tfrac{7}{3}s_4$. Thus the two different formulas for $F$ agree on the domain of $F$. The reasoning in this example is generalized in Theorem 1 below.

The corner number of a condensed tableau can be important because this is the number obtained when the objective function is evaluated at the basic solution of the tableau:

$$F(\text{basic solution}) = \text{corner number}.$$

For instance in the last tableau, $F(0, \tfrac{2}{3}, \tfrac{13}{3}, 0) = \tfrac{14}{3}$. We have to be careful, however; if one or more of the constants $\beta_1, \ldots, \beta_m$ are negative, the basic solution is not a feasible solution of the LP problem, and the corner number may have no significance for the problem. More on this point later.

We now formulate the basic theorem on pivoting tableaux of form (2).

**Theorem 1.** *Let tableau (2) be displayed as*

|         | $\cdots$ | $k_q$ | $\cdots$ | $k_s$ | $\cdots$ |  |
|---------|----------|-------------|----------|-----------------|----------|---------|
| $\vdots$ |  | $\vdots$ |  | $\vdots$ |  | $\vdots$ |
| $j_r$ | $\cdots$ | $\alpha_{rq}$ | $\cdots$ | $\boxed{\alpha_{rs}}$ | $\cdots$ | $\beta_r$ |
| $\vdots$ |  | $\vdots$ |  | $\vdots$ |  | $\vdots$ |
| $F$ | $\cdots$ | $\gamma_q$ | $\cdots$ | $\gamma_s$ | $\cdots$ | $\delta$ |

$\qquad\qquad (2)$

*where $\alpha_{rs} \neq 0$ (and $q \neq s$). Let*

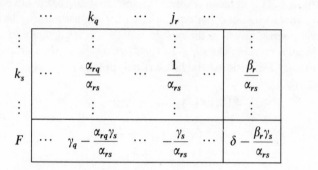

$$(2')$$

*be the result of pivoting (2) at $\alpha_{rs}$ as described in Theorem 6 of Chapter 1, but with the pivoting rules extended to the objective row. Then the LP problems represented by (2) and (2') are the same in the following sense.*

(i) *The feasible regions are the same, and*

(ii) *the formulas for F in (2) and (2') agree on this common feasible region. In fact, the formulas agree at each solution of either the linear system of (2) or of (2'), whether or not all the components of such a solution are nonnegative.*

*Proof.* We know (Chapter 1, Theorems 3 and 6) that the linear systems of (2) and (2') have exactly the same solutions. Moreover, by Definition 1, those solutions with nonnegative components are the feasible solutions of either LP problem (2) or LP problem (2'). Thus assertion (i) is proved.

It is now clear that there only remains the proof of the final statement in (ii). To this end we let $(t_1, \ldots, t_{n+m})$ be an arbitrary solution of either (and therefore both) of the linear systems. Then the displayed row of (2) gives the equation

$$t_{j_r} + \sum_{q \neq s} \alpha_{rq} t_{k_q} + \alpha_{rs} t_{k_s} = \beta_r.$$

Further, according to the formula for $F$ in (2),

$$F(t_1, \ldots, t_{n+m}) + \sum_{q \neq s} \gamma_q t_{k_q} + \gamma_s t_{k_s} = \delta.$$

Multiplying the first equation by $-\gamma_s/\alpha_{rs}$, and adding the result to the last equation eliminates $t_{k_s}$ and yields

$$F(t_1, \ldots, t_{n+m}) + \sum_{q \neq s} \left(\gamma_q - \frac{\alpha_{rq}\gamma_s}{\alpha_{rs}}\right) t_{k_q} - \frac{\gamma_s}{\alpha_{rs}} t_{j_r} = \delta - \frac{\beta_r \gamma_s}{\alpha_{rs}}.$$

But this is precisely the result obtainable by applying the objective row of (2') to $(t_1, \ldots, t_{n+m})$. It follows that both formulas for $F$ assign the same value to $(t_1, \ldots, t_{n+m})$, as was to be shown.  $\square$

We remark that the last sentence of (ii) above is not required in a reasonable interpretation of the phrase "same LP problem". However, this stronger statement will be needed in the proof of the important Theorem 9. Also to be significant later is the following result, Theorem 2. The symbol $\binom{n+m}{m}$ appearing in the theorem represents the number of subsets with $m$ elements, of a set with $n + m$ elements.

**Theorem 2.** *If a sequence of pivoting operations (of the type in Theorem 1) leads from tableau (2) to a tableau with the same basis as (2), then this tableau is identical to (2). There are at most $\binom{n+m}{m}$ different tableaux obtainable from (2) by repeated pivoting, arbitrarily many times. (In both of these statements, tableaux differing only by a permutation of the rows or columns are considered identical.)*

*Proof.* The first assertion follows immediately from results of Chapter 1 (Theorems 3, 5, and 6) if we regard $F$ as just an additional variable, remaining basic throughout the pivoting sequence. From this point of view the final tableau of the sequence has the same $m + 1$ basic variables as tableau (2), and is therefore identical to it.

To prove the second assertion of the theorem, we observe that the set of variables $\{x_1, \ldots, x_{n+m}\}$ has $\binom{n+m}{m}$ subsets with $m$ elements. Therefore, there are at most $\binom{n+m}{m}$ bases obtainable by repeated pivoting, beginning with (2). The assertion now follows immediately from what has already been proved.  □

We now define and discuss the type of LP problem to which the algorithm SIMPLEX will be applicable.

**Definition 2.** An LP problem is in *simplex form* if it can be represented (Definition 1) by a tableau of form (2) with all (right-hand) constants non-negative, that is, by a tableau of the form

$$
\begin{array}{c|ccc|c}
 & k_1 & \cdots & k_n & \\
\hline
j_1 & \alpha_{11} & \cdots & \alpha_{1n} & \beta_1 \\
\vdots & \vdots & & \vdots & \vdots \\
j_m & \alpha_{m1} & \cdots & \alpha_{mn} & \beta_m \\
\hline
F & \gamma_1 & \cdots & \gamma_n & \delta
\end{array}
\quad, \quad \beta_1, \ldots, \beta_m \geq 0. \tag{3}
$$

This is called a *simplex tableau*.

Expressed without tableaux, an LP problem is in simplex form if the following four conditions are satisfied:

(i) There are nonnegativity constraints on all the variables.

(ii) The only other constraints are equalities, and these form a linear system in basic form.
(iii) The objective function, to be maximized, is expressed in terms of only the nonbasic variables of the linear system.
(iv) All the constants of the linear system are nonnegative.

Problems in simplex form arise most naturally from LP problems in primal form (Chapter 2, Definition 1) with nonnegative constants; the enlarged problem (Chapter 2, Definition 6) is then in simplex form. The production problem (Chapter 2) is an important example of this. On the other hand, the diet problem (also Chapter 2) and many other LP problems are beyond the scope of this chapter. (Such problems are treated in Chapter 4.)

Given an arbitrary LP problem, we can always obtain conditions (i) through (iii) by first passing to the primal form replacement (Chapter 2, Definition 3) and then to the enlarged problem. Condition (iv), however, is then "beyond our control." To add to the argument that condition (iv) is the only truly crucial condition for simplex form, we remark that (iii) is obtainable by a computation once (i) and (ii) hold. More precisely, suppose that an LP problem satisfies (i) and (ii), that the objective function is expressed in terms of the variables of the linear system of (ii), but that one or more basic variables appear in the expression. These basic variables can then be eliminated by replacing each by its formula, found in the linear system, in terms of nonbasic variables. (This remark will have an application in the next chapter.)

An obvious but important property of a problem in simplex form is its *feasibility*. Indeed, the basic solution of the system of equality constraints is one feasible solution. This is clear because in the basic solution the value of every variable is either zero or one of the nonnegative constants. Thus, there are only two possible outcomes to an LP problem in simplex form: The objective function either has a maximum value or is unbounded above. (Definition 5 of Chapter 2 and the discussion immediately preceding are relevant here. The proof of this two-outcomes theorem comes in Theorem 10 at the end of this chapter.)

In the absence of condition (iv) of simplex form, an LP problem can easily be infeasible. Let us consider, for example,

|     | 1   | 2   |     |
|-----|-----|-----|-----|
| 3   | 0   | 3   | $-1$ |
| 4   | $-2$ | $-5$ | 2   |
|     |     |     |     |

the objective function being irrelevant. The infeasibility is evident because the equation $x_3 + 3x_2 = -1$ cannot be satisfied by any nonnegative values of $x_2$ and $x_3$. The following less obvious example is left as an exercise:

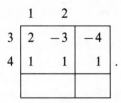

Given a simplex tableau, not only is a feasible solution, namely, the basic solution, on display, but so is a *feasible value of the objective function.* We make this precise in the next definition and lemma.

**Definition 3.** Given any LP problem, a number $\delta$ is a *feasible value of the objective function* if there exists a feasible solution of the problem, evaluated at which the objective function has the value $\delta$. In other words, $\delta$ belongs to the range of the objective function.

In terms of this definition, solving an LP maximization problem entails either finding the largest feasible value of the objective function, or showing that there are arbitrarily large feasible values, or showing that there are no feasible values at all.

**Lemma 1.** *The corner number in a simplex tableau is a feasible value of the objective function. More specifically, the basic solution of the tableau is a feasible solution, and the value of the objective function at this feasible solution is the corner number.*

*Proof* (A repeat of previous observations.) In the notation of Definition 2, the basic solution is the $(n + m)$-tuple defined by the assignment of values

$$x_{k_1} = \cdots = x_{k_n} = 0, \qquad x_{j_1} = \beta_1, \ldots, x_{j_m} = \beta_m.$$

This $(n + m)$-tuple is clearly a feasible solution. Since the objective row of (3) reads

$$F(x_1, \ldots, x_{n+m}) + \gamma_1 x_{k_1} + \cdots + \gamma_n x_{k_n} = \delta,$$

the value of $F$ at this feasible solution is $\delta$, as required.    $\square$

This proof should be clearly contrasted with the following faulty reasoning. In the example

|   | 1 | 2 |   |
|---|---|---|---|
| 3 | $-4$ | 0 | $-1$ |
| 4 | 0 | 3 | 10 |
| $F$ | 2 | $-1$ | 8 |

,

$F(x_1, x_2, x_3, x_4) = 8 - 2x_1 + x_2$. Therefore, assigning the value 0 to both $x_1$

and $x_2$ produces the value 8 of $F$. Therefore 8 is a feasible value of $F$.(?) The argument is incorrect because the domain of $F$ is contained in $R^4$, so it is not sufficient to consider the values of only two of the variables. Indeed, the values $x_1 = x_2 = 0$ lead, via the first equality constraint, to the value $x_3 = -1$. Thus there is no feasible 4-tuple with first and second components equal to zero. Nevertheless, it would be another mistake to conclude that 8 is not a feasible value of $F$! For instance it is easy to check that $(1, 2, 3, 4)$ is a feasible solution, and that $F(1, 2, 3, 4) = 8$.

For an example in which the corner number is not a feasible value, we change the objective row of the last tableau from

$$F \begin{array}{|ccc|} \hline 2 & -1 & 8 \\ \hline \end{array} \quad \text{to} \quad F \begin{array}{|ccc|} \hline 2 & 1 & 8 \\ \hline \end{array}.$$

Then $F(x_1, x_2, x_3, x_4) = 8 - (2x_1 + x_2)$. For any feasible solution $(s_1, s_2, s_3, s_4)$ it is of course true that $s_1 \geq 0$ and $s_2 \geq 0$. Therefore $2s_1 + s_2 \geq 0$ and $F(s_1, s_2, s_3, s_4) \leq 8$. But, as mentioned above, $s_1$ and $s_2$ cannot both be zero if $(s_1, s_2, s_3, s_4)$ is feasible. It follows that $F(s_1, s_2, s_3, s_4) < 8$. Hence, 8 is now not a feasible value of $F$; it is, in fact, an unattainable upper bound of $F$. Thus, for a condensed tableau that is not a simplex tableau, the corner number can be, but need not be, a feasible value of the objective function. Fortunately, we avoid this problem when dealing with simplex tableaux.

We are now well prepared for the following important result. It provides a condition on a simplex tableau that implies that the LP problem represented by the tableau is solved. In this theorem and elsewhere in discussing SIMPLEX, the reader should carefully distinguish between *positive* and *nonnegative*. The difference is that zero is nonnegative but not positive.

**Theorem 3** (Optimality Theorem). *Suppose every objective entry of a simplex tableau is nonnegative. Then the basic solution of the tableau is an OFS., and the corner number is the maximum value of the objective function.*

*Proof.* With the notation of the general simplex tableau (3), we let $(s_1, \ldots, s_{n+m})$ be an arbitrary feasible solution. Then

$$F(s_1, \ldots, s_{n+m}) = \delta - (\gamma_1 s_{k_1} + \cdots + \gamma_n s_{k_n}).$$

By hypothesis $\gamma_1, \ldots, \gamma_n$ are all nonnegative, and by the nonnegativity constraints so are $s_{k_1}, \ldots, s_{k_n}$. It follows that $F(s_1, \ldots, s_{n+m}) \leq \delta$. In words, $\delta$ is an upper bound of $F$. On the other hand, by Lemma 1, the basic solution is feasible, and the corresponding value of $F$ is exactly $\delta$. The conclusion of the theorem follows.   $\square$

It is possible for the conclusion of the Optimality Theorem to hold for a simplex tableau *without* every objective entry being nonnegative. For the reason given in the next paragraph, this fact is not important. Still, it is interesting enough to warrant an example:

|   | 1 | 2 |   |
|---|---|---|---|
| 3 | $-1$ | 2 | 0 |
| 4 | 8 | 9 | 10 |
| $F$ | 1 | $-1$ | 5 |

It is clear that the basic solution of this tableau is $(0, 0, 0, 10)$, that $F(0, 0, 0, 10) = 5$, and that $F(s_1, s_2, s_3, s_4) = 5 - (s_1 - s_2)$ for an arbitrary feasible solution. Hence, one way to prove that max $F = F(0, 0, 0, 10) = 5$ is to show that $s_1 - s_2 \geq 0$. This is a consequence of the first equality constraint together with the nonnegativity constraints. The details are left as an exercise.

One of the most important and impressive facts about SIMPLEX is the following. If the objective function of an LP problem in simplex form has a maximum value, SIMPLEX "essentially always" leads to a final tableau in which all objective entries are nonnegative. We shall clarify this statement later, but we can easily illustrate it with the last example. For that tableau SIMPLEX instructs, as we shall see later, that we pivot at 2. This produces the tableau

|   | 1 | 3 |   |
|---|---|---|---|
| 2 | $-\frac{1}{2}$ | $\frac{1}{2}$ | 0 |
| 4 | $\frac{25}{2}$ | $-\frac{9}{2}$ | 10 |
| $F$ | $\frac{1}{2}$ | $\frac{1}{2}$ | 5 |

to which Theorem 3 applies. The conclusion is that max $F = F(0, 0, 0, 10) = 5$, the same result reached by the ad hoc reasoning in the last paragraph!

We defer discussion of how SIMPLEX chooses pivots and solves LP problems in favor of a (perhaps) more immediate question: How can one recognize the other possible outcome of an LP problem in simplex form, namely, that the objective function is unbounded above? If such a situation is recognized, there is, of course, no reason to do any pivoting.

Let us consider the following example before the general theorem:

|   | 2 | 4 | 5 |   |
|---|---|---|---|---|
| 1 | $-5$ | 6 | 9 | 2 |
| 3 | $-4$ | 4 | 8 | 3 |
| 6 | 0 | 1 | $-7$ | 4 |
| $F$ | $-8$ | $-9$ | 3 | $-10$ |

There is a negative objective entry, $-8$, with no positive number in its column. This pattern implies that $F$ is unbounded above, as the following argument demonstrates. We choose a number $t > 0$ and consider the feasible solution with

$$x_2 = t, \qquad x_4 = 0, \qquad x_5 = 0, \qquad \text{(nonbasic variables)};$$

$$x_1 = 5t + 2, \qquad x_3 = 4t + 3, \qquad x_6 = 4, \qquad \text{(basic variables)}.$$

What we have done is let all nonbasic variables have the value zero, except the variable of the "pattern column." This variable is assigned the positive value $t$. The values of the basic variables are then determined by the equality constraints. These latter values have clearly turned out to be nonnegative for any $t > 0$. The critical reason is that the nonpositive column entries $-5$, $-4$, and 0 have led to nonnegative coefficients of $t$, namely 5, 4, and 0. Next, the objective row yields $F(5t + 2, t, 4t + 3, 0, 0, 4) = 8t - 10$. (The positive coefficient 8 results from the negative objective entry $-8$). Finally, since $8t - 10$ is a feasible value of $F$ no matter how large $t$ may be, it is clear that $F$ is unbounded above, as asserted.

It is instructive to see how the argument fails if one of the column entries above $-8$ is replaced by a positive number. If, for example, $-5$ is replaced by 5, and we choose values of the nonbasic variables exactly as before, we are led to the 6-tuple $(-5t + 2, t, 4t + 3, 0, 0, 4)$. This is now a feasible solution only for $0 \le t \le \frac{2}{5}$. The corresponding feasible value of $F$, still $8t - 10$, is now at most $8(\frac{2}{5}) - 10$.

It is not difficult to generalize the reasoning of the (original) example and obtain the following theorem.

**Theorem 4** (Unboundedness Theorem). *If a simplex tableau has a negative objective entry with no positive entry in its column, then the objective function is unbounded above.*

*Proof.* The hypotheses imply a tableau of the form

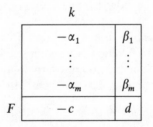

with $c > 0$; $\alpha_1 \ge 0, \ldots, \alpha_m \ge 0$; $\beta_1 \ge 0, \ldots, \beta_m \ge 0$. For $t > 0$ we choose a solution of the system of equality constraints as follows:

(i) The variable $x_k$ has the value $t$.
(ii) All other nonbasic variables have the value zero.

The basic variables then have values $\alpha_1 t + \beta_1, \ldots, \alpha_m t + \beta_m$ in some order. Since all $\alpha$'s and $\beta$'s are nonnegative, this solution of the linear system of constraints is a feasible solution of the LP problem under consideration, regardless of the size of $t$. The value of $F$ at this feasible solution is $ct + d$.

Since $c > 0$ and $t$ can be arbitrarily large, $ct + d$ can also be arbitrarily large. Hence $F$ is unbounded above.    $\square$

We have now learned the two simplex tableau patterns that signal a solved LP problem, namely, the *optimality pattern* of Theorem 3 (all objective entries nonnegative) and the *unboundedness pattern* of Theorem 4 (a negative objective entry with no positive number in its column). Therefore, we now suppose that we have a simplex tableau possessing neither of these patterns. The absence of the first pattern means that there is at least one negative objective entry; the absence of the second implies that every negative objective entry has at least one positive number in its column. SIMPLEX requires that we choose such a positive number as a pivot: again, *a positive pivot above a negative objective entry.*

The desirability of pivoting a simplex tableau according to this scheme depends on two simple facts, which we shall prove. First, whenever the scheme is followed, the corner number of the tableau generated is greater than or equal to that of the tableau being pivoted. Second, the scheme can always be implemented in such a way that the new tableau generated is again a simplex tableau. (We shall soon be more specific.) If this is done, the new corner number, like the old, is a feasible value of the objective function. Putting these facts together, we conclude that our pivoting scheme, correctly implemented, generates a sequence of *nondecreasing feasible values.* Since we wish to maximize the objective function, this is desirable, at least when "nondecreasing" is actually "increasing."

We now have some understanding of how pivoting can produce progress in solving an LP problem in simplex form. Whether such progress leads to a complete solution remains to be seen. Our immediate goal is to prove the first of the two facts described above. We add a little information for later use.

**Theorem 5.** *Let T be a simplex tableau containing neither the optimality pattern nor the unboundedness pattern. Then T contains at least one negative objective entry, and every such entry has at least one positive number in its column. If T is pivoted at any such positive number, the corner number of the resulting tableau is greater than or equal to that of T. Equality prevails if and only if the constant in the row of the chosen pivot is zero.*

*Proof.* The first sentence of the conclusion is just a rewording of the hypothesis. To prove the main assertions, we display T as

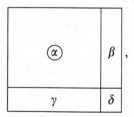

where $\alpha > 0$, $\beta \geq 0$, and $\gamma < 0$. If T is pivoted at $\alpha$ as indicated, the new corner number is $\delta - \beta\gamma/\alpha$. The conditions on $\alpha$, $\beta$, and $\gamma$ imply that $-\beta\gamma/\alpha \geq 0$. Therefore $\delta - \beta\gamma/\alpha \geq \delta$ as asserted. Equality holds here if and only if $\beta\gamma/\alpha = 0$. Since $\gamma \neq 0$, this is equivalent to $\beta = 0$.  $\square$

We now come to the problem of preserving simplex form while following the scheme "positive pivot above a negative objective entry." What we show is that in any column containing one or more positive entries, there is always a choice of positive pivot, that ensures that the new tableau again has only nonnegative constants; the objective entry at the bottom of the column is irrelevant to the discussion. Let us begin with an example, namely, the simplex tableau (fragment)

| | |
|---|---|
| 2 | 8 |
| $-4$ | 5 |
| 6 | 12 |
| 0 | 7 |
| | |

We study whether to pivot at 2 or at 6. (By Theorem 5, if the relevant objective entry is negative, the new corner number will be greater than the present one, regardless of whether 2 or 6 is chosen. However, for the purpose of preserving simplex form the choice of 2 or 6 is crucial.)

If we choose 2 as pivot, the "replacements" for the constants 8, 5, 12, 7 are

$$\frac{8}{2}, \quad 5 - \frac{(-4)(8)}{2}, \quad 12 - \frac{(6)(8)}{2}, \quad 7 - \frac{(0)(8)}{2},$$

respectively. If 6 is chosen, the new constants are

$$8 - \frac{(2)(12)}{6}, \quad 5 - \frac{(-4)(12)}{6}, \quad \frac{12}{6}, \quad 7 - \frac{(0)(12)}{6}.$$

Six of these eight numbers are nonnegative by their general form: a nonnegative constant divided by a positive pivot, or an original nonnegative constant minus a negative or zero term. Only $12 - (6)(8)/2$ and $8 - (2)(12)/6$ require a second glance. The first of these is negative; the second is positive. Thus pivoting at 2 destroys simplex form; pivoting at 6 preserves it.

The main point to be made is that we can efficiently determine the correct pivot in advance, both in the example and generally. In the example let us divide the inequality $8 - (2)(12)/6 > 0$ by 2 and obtain $\frac{8}{2} - \frac{12}{6} > 0$, which we rewrite as

$$\frac{12}{6} < \frac{8}{2}.$$

In this form of our inequality two ratios are compared. Each ratio has a "pivot candidate" as denominator and the constant in its row as numerator. *Such ratios are called θ-ratios, and apparently the smallest θ-ratio for the column determines the pivot.* Our study of the example has indicated that θ-ratios are needed only for the positive entries of the column being considered. The reason is that the replacement for a constant opposite a negative or zero column entry will automatically be nonnegative.

Before stating a formal definition and theorem let us observe that there can be a tie for minimum θ-ratio in a given column. For example, in the tableau

| | |
|---|---|
| 2 | 8 |
| −4 | 5 |
| 6 | 12 |
| 9 | 18 |
| | |

the θ-ratios for the displayed column are $\frac{8}{2}$, $\frac{12}{6}$, and $\frac{18}{9}$. The minimum of these is either $\frac{12}{6}$ or $\frac{18}{9}$. Pivoting at 6 produces the constants 4, 13, 2, 0; choosing 9 yields 4, 13, 0, 2. Thus it appears that any pivot candidate "participating in the tie" for minimum θ-ratio can successfully be chosen as pivot. (Such a pivot always produces at least one zero among the new constants. This may be a nuisance because a zero constant can affect the next pivoting operation in the manner described in Theorem 5. We return to this matter later. As mentioned in Chapter 1, a basic solution is called *degenerate* if some basic variable has the value zero.)

Further examples of simplex entries with minimum θ-ratio in their columns are circled in the following tableaux:

| | | | | | | | | | | |
|---|---|---|---|---|---|---|---|---|---|---|
| ②| 1 | | ② | 10 | | | | | −2 | |
| 3 | 2 | | ③ | 15 | | ③ | 0 | | −3 | |
| −4 | 3 | | −4 | 20 | | | | | −4 | |
| 5 | 4 | | 5 | 30 | | | | | ⑤ | |
| | | | | | | | | | | |

Our formal definition and theorem are the following.

**Definition 4.** Given a positive entry (not in the objective row and not in the constant column) of a simplex tableau, the associated *θ-ratio* is the quotient of the constant in the same row divided by the given entry. [In the notation of the general simplex tableau (3): If $\alpha_{rs} > 0$ for a row index $r$ $(1 \leq r \leq m)$ and a column index $s$ $(1 \leq s \leq n)$, then the $\theta$-ratio for the entry $\alpha_{rs}$ is $\beta_r / \alpha_{rs}$.]

**Theorem 6.** *If a simplex tableau is pivoted at a positive entry for which the $\theta$-ratio is a column minimum, then the resulting tableau is again a simplex tableau.*

*Proof.* We display the given simplex tableau as follows:

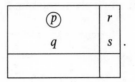

Here $p$ is the chosen pivot, $r$ is the constant in its row, $s$ is any other constant, and $q$ is the entry in the row of $s$ and the column of $p$. Given that the $\theta$-ratio for $p$ is a column minimum, we shall show that the replacements for $r$ and $s$ are nonnegative. We shall then know that *every* constant has a nonnegative replacement, and the proof will be complete.

By the assumptions of the theorem $p > 0$, $r \geq 0$, and $s \geq 0$. The replacement for $r$ is $r/p$, which is clearly nonnegative. To finish the proof, we must show that $s - qr/p$ is nonnegative. For this we distinguish two cases: $q \leq 0$ and $q > 0$. In the first case $-qr/p \geq 0$, and therefore $s - qr/p \geq s \geq 0$. In the second case the $\theta$-ratio for $q$ is defined, and the minimum $\theta$-ratio property of $p$ yields $r/p \leq s/q$. Multiplying this inequality by the positive number $q$, we obtain $qr/p \leq s$, or $s - qr/p \geq 0$ as required.   $\square$

We are now (finally!) ready to define SIMPLEX formally. We present the algorithm first as an ordinary list of written instructions, and then in a diagrammatic form known as a flowchart (Fig. 2). The first form is a little more formal and complete, whereas the flowchart provides a quicker overall view. We shall prefer the flowchart. There are some informative assertions mixed in with the instructions of the algorithm, but all such assertions have already been proved.

**Definition 5** (SIMPLEX). The algorithm SIMPLEX is defined for LP problems in simplex form (Definition 2). Expressed in terms of the tableau representation (Definition 1) of such a problem, the steps of the algorithm are the following:

(i) Determine whether there is a negative objective entry in the simplex tableau. If not, conclude that the basic solution of the tableau is an OFS and that the corner number is the maximum value of the objective function. If so, go on to step (ii).

(ii) Determine whether every negative objective entry (at least one is present) has a positive number in its column. If not, conclude that the objective function is unbounded above. If so, go on to step (iii).

(iii)  Select any negative objective entry.
(iv)  In the column of the previous choice select a positive entry (at least one is present) for which the $\theta$-ratio is a column minimum. (If there is more than one entry with minimum $\theta$-ratio, choose any such entry.)
(v)  Pivot the tableau at the entry selected in the previous step. The resulting tableau is again a simplex tableau representing the given LP problem. Go to step (i) with the new tableau.

*Note*: There exist several variations of this definition, of which we now mention two. In most practical applications of the simplex algorithm, there is no unboundedness search of the type described in (ii). The time that would be required is usually better spent by going on to the pivoting. If unboundedness ever occurs, it is detected only in a column intended for pivoting. In another SIMPLEX variation, formerly common in applications, the choice of negative objective entry is restricted to one of greatest absolute value. (See Problem 20.)

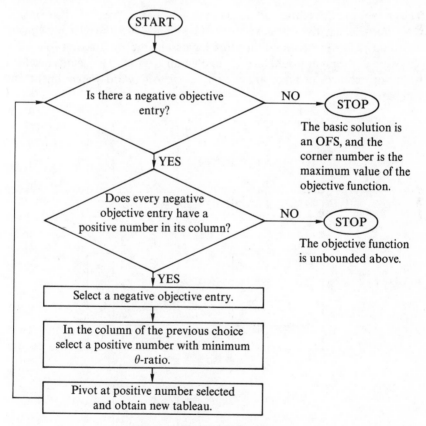

**Figure 2.** SIMPLEX flowchart.

An important fact about Definition 5 is that each of steps (iii) and (iv) can allow more than one choice. As a consequence, there are normally many ways to follow the SIMPLEX instructions in a given LP problem. We shall soon discuss augmenting SIMPLEX by some *choice–deciding rules*.

Perhaps the main question suggested by Definition 5 is whether SIMPLEX always terminates. The alternative would be to "go endlessly around the loop" in the flowchart, always getting "yes" answers. We settle this question later in the chapter with the help of choice-deciding rules.

For our first example for the SIMPLEX flowchart, let us consider the simplex tableau

|   | 1 | 2 |   |
|---|---|---|---|
| 3 | 1 | 3 | 4 |
| 4 | $-1$ | 2 | 0 |
| 5 | 1 | 4 | 5 |
| F | $-3$ | $-2$ | 0 |

The answer to both of the questions in the flowchart is "yes," so the next step is to choose a negative objective entry. If we choose $-3$, the relevant $\theta$-ratios are $\frac{4}{1}$ and $\frac{5}{1}$. The pivot would therefore have to be the 1 in the first row. If we choose $-2$, the pivot would be the 2 in column 2, row 2. The details resulting from both choices of pivot are shown below. Afterward we comment and compare.

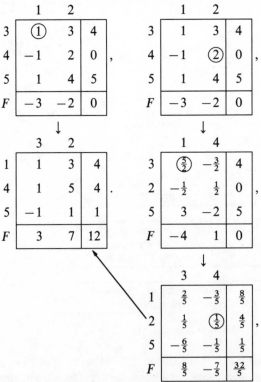

Choosing 1 as initial pivot clearly leads to easier and shorter calculations. Two general observations are relevant here. First, pivoting always requires division by the pivot. Therefore, hand computations tend to be easiest when the pivot is a 1. Second, as mentioned in Theorem 5, pivoting in the row of a zero constant produces a tableau with no increase in the corner number. In a significant sense, no progress is made. From this viewpoint we expect pivoting at 2 to initiate a lengthier computation than pivoting at 1.

Choosing 2 as pivot in this example does perhaps have one dubious advantage: One thereby obtains a substantial workout practicing SIMPLEX. In any case, a unique final tableau is reached, and the conclusion to the problem is that max $F = F(4, 0, 0, 4, 1) = 12$.

When SIMPLEX produces a tableau with the same corner number as that of the preceding tableau, we say that the algorithm *stalls*. Stalling one or more times before termination is a common phenomenon in SIMPLEX solutions of practical LP problems. Therefore we present one more (nonpractical) example, some accompanying remarks, and a simple theorem on stalling. The example and remarks are as follows.

|   | 1 | 2 | 3 |   |
|---|---|---|---|---|
| 4 | 1 | −1 | ① | 2 |
| 5 | 2 | −2 | 3 | 6 |
| 6 | −2 | 9 | −10 | 1 |
| F | 3 | 0 | −1 | 0 |

Must pivot in column 3.
Tie for minimum $\theta$-ratio in this column. Choose 1 as pivot; reject 3.

|   | 1 | 2 | 4 |   |
|---|---|---|---|---|
| 3 | 1 | −1 | 1 | 2 |
| 5 | −1 | ① | −3 | 0 |
| 6 | 8 | −1 | 10 | 21 |
| F | 4 | −1 | 1 | 2 |

A zero replaces the constant in the row of the previous rejected pivot candidate. Current pivot must be in row of zero constant.

|   | 1 | 5 | 4 |   |
|---|---|---|---|---|
| 3 | 0 | 1 | −2 | 2 |
| 2 | −1 | 1 | −3 | 0 |
| 6 | 7 | 1 | ⑦ | 21 |
| F | 3 | 1 | −2 | 2 |

Same corner number as in previous tableau. Also same basic solution, namely, (0, 0, 2, 0, 0, 21), as in previous tableau (even though the basis is different!).

|   | 1 | 5 | 6 |   |
|---|---|---|---|---|
| 3 |   |   |   | 8 |
| 2 |   |   |   | 9 |
| 4 |   |   |   | 3 |
| F | 5 | $\frac{9}{7}$ | $\frac{2}{7}$ | 8 |

Optimality reached.

Our theorem provides three equivalent formulations of stalling.

**Theorem 7.** *For two consecutive tableaux occurring in an application of SIM-PLEX, the following statements are equivalent.*

(i)  *The corner numbers are equal.*
(ii)  *The basic solutions are equal.*
(iii)  *The constant in the pivot row of the prior tableau is zero.*

*Proof.* We already know (Theorem 5) that (i) and (iii) are equivalent. We shall conclude the proof by showing that (iii) implies (ii), and (ii) implies (i).

Assuming (iii), we can represent the earlier tableau by

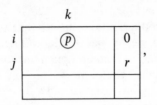

where $p$ is the pivot, $x_i$ is about to be replaced in the basis by $x_k$, $x_j$ is any basic variable other than $x_i$, and $r$ is the value of $x_j$ in the basic solution. The variables $x_i$ and $x_k$ both have the value zero in the basic solution. The succeeding tableau is

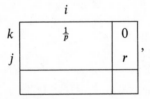

the constant column being exactly the same as before. Thus, in the basic solution of this tableau, each of $x_i$, $x_j$, and $x_k$ have the same values as before. It is therefore clear that *every* variable has the same value in both basic solutions; that is, the basic solutions of the two tableaux are the same. Thus (iii) implies (ii).

Finally, we assume (ii): Our two consecutive tableaux have the same basic solution. The objective function formulas of these two tableaux assign the same value to this basic solution (Theorem 1). Furthermore (Lemma 1), the value assigned by each formula is the corner number of its tableau. Thus (i) follows. □

We now begin to discuss the interesting and important question of termination. The phrase "SIMPLEX terminates" means that a tableau is generated with one of the two patterns leading to "stop" in the flowchart. Such a tableau can appropriately be called a *final tableau*. The alternative to termination, if possible, is the generation of an infinite sequence of tableaux with neither of the two patterns.

We shall see that there is enough latitude in Definition 5, namely, in steps (iii) and (iv), to allow examples of nontermination! Indeed, we shall shortly present a specific simplex tableau, together with some choice-deciding rules for selecting pivots. With this tableau as the initial tableau, and with these rules added to the existing rules of Definition 5, SIMPLEX generates a never-ending sequence of tableaux.

The possibility of termination failure in SIMPLEX is perhaps disappointing, but the remaining facts are positive. First, SIMPLEX very rarely fails to terminate in practical problems (as opposed to cleverly devised examples), no matter how the choices in steps (iii) and (iv) are made. Second, there is enough latitude in these steps to allow the existence also of "good" choice-deciding rules: SIMPLEX augmented by such rules *always* terminates (Definition 6 and Theorem 9 to come).

Our example of nontermination is one of perpetual stalling, created in 1955 by Beale [1]. The initial tableau is

$$
\text{I:}\quad
\begin{array}{c|cccc|c}
 & 1 & 2 & 3 & 4 & \\
\hline
5 & \frac{1}{4} & -8 & -1 & 9 & 0 \\
6 & \frac{1}{2} & -12 & -\frac{1}{2} & 3 & 0 \\
7 & 0 & 0 & 1 & 0 & 1 \\
\hline
F & -\frac{3}{4} & 20 & -\frac{1}{2} & 6 & 0
\end{array}\quad,
$$

and the choice-deciding rules for selecting pivots are as follows:

*Step* (iii) *Rule*: The smallest objective entry determines the pivot column. (In Beale's example there will be a unique smallest objective entry in every tableau produced; in other examples this rule could be unclear.)

*Step* (iv) *Rule*: Break all ties for minimum $\theta$-ratio by choosing as pivot the "candidate" with smallest row heading.

Let us illustrate the operation of these new rules on tableau I. Since $-\frac{3}{4} < -\frac{1}{2}$, the pivot must come from column 1. In this column both $\frac{1}{4}$ and $\frac{1}{2}$ have minimum $\theta$-ratio. We are required to choose $\frac{1}{4}$ as pivot because the row heading 5 is less than row heading 6.

Now let the tableaux following I be denoted II, III, and so on. The result is that no final tableau is produced, and *tableau VII is identical to tableau I*. (The columns of VII do not appear in the same order as in I, but we continue to disregard such trivial differences between tableaux.) As an aid and incentive to the reader to undertake the necessary computation, tableaux III and V, together with correct choices of pivot, are shown:

$$
\text{III:}\quad
\begin{array}{c|cccc|c}
 & 5 & 6 & 3 & 4 & \\
\hline
1 & -12 & 8 & \boxed{8} & -84 & 0 \\
2 & -\frac{1}{2} & \frac{1}{4} & \frac{3}{8} & -\frac{15}{4} & 0 \\
7 & 0 & 0 & 1 & 0 & 1 \\
\hline
F & 1 & 1 & -2 & 18 & 0
\end{array}\quad,
$$

|   | 5 | 6 | 1 | 2 | |
|---|---|---|---|---|---|
| 3 | ② | $-6$ | $-\frac{5}{2}$ | $56$ | 0 |
| V:    4 | $\frac{1}{3}$ | $-\frac{2}{3}$ | $-\frac{1}{4}$ | $\frac{16}{3}$ | 0 |
| 7 | $-2$ | $6$ | $\frac{5}{2}$ | $-56$ | 1 |
| F | $-1$ | $1$ | $-\frac{1}{2}$ | $16$ | 0 |

Since tableaux I and VII are identical, it follows that a nonending sequence of the form

$$I, \dots, VI, I, \dots, VI, \dots$$

is generated: an infinitely repeated cycle of six tableaux. (We are assuming, of course, that Beale's two extra rules remain in effect; below we free ourselves of them.) Thus it is demonstrated that SIMPLEX need not terminate.

Before leaving this remarkable example, we assume that the extra rules are discarded. The most sensible choice of pivot in tableau I is then the entry 1 in the third row. This choice avoids stalling and produces a tableau with corner number $\frac{1}{2}$. It then requires only one further pivot to reach optimality and the conclusion that max $F = \frac{5}{4}$. Thus, depending on the route through SIMPLEX, both termination and nontermination can occur in the same example.

The following theorem shows that some properties of Beale's example hold in general when termination fails. (Problem 26 sheds some additional light.)

**Theorem 8.** *Let $m$ and $n$, respectively, be the number of basic and nonbasic variables in a simplex tableau. Then after at most $\binom{n+m}{m}$ iterations SIMPLEX either terminates or produces a tableau identical to a prior one. If an infinite sequence of tableaux is generated, the corner numbers are eventually all equal.*

*Proof.* By Theorem 2 no more than $\binom{n+m}{m}$ different tableaux can be generated by SIMPLEX (or indeed by arbitrary pivoting). If the algorithm goes through as many as $\binom{n+m}{m}$ iterations, $\binom{n+m}{m} + 1$ tableaux thereby appear. Consequently, at least two are identical. The first assertion of the theorem now follows.

Finally, let us assume that SIMPLEX produces an infinite sequence of tableaux. Since only finitely many *different* tableaux can be produced, we can choose a tableau that recurs infinitely often. We then consider any two successive occurrences of the chosen tableau and the sequence of corner numbers leading from one to the other. Since this sequence is nondecreasing (Theorem 5), and since the first and last members of the sequence are the same, all must be equal. Hence, beginning with the first occurrence of the chosen tableau (if not earlier), all the corner numbers are equal.    □

**Corollary** (Elementary SIMPLEX Termination Theorem). *Suppose in an application of SIMPLEX the pivot in every tableau has a nonzero constant in its row. Then the algorithm terminates in at most $\binom{n+m}{m}$ iterations.*

*Proof.* The hypothesis implies (by Theorem 5) that the corner numbers are strictly increasing. Hence no tableau produced can be the same as a prior one. Thus the conclusion follows from the preceding theorem.    □

We have referred to this result as an "elementary" termination theorem because the hypothesis is extremely strong, and the conclusion follows so easily. It generally cannot be known in advance whether a given SIMPLEX problem will lead to a "nonstalling" pivot in every tableau generated. Therefore the corollary has little if any applicability. Fortunately, practical problems almost invariably terminate whether or not such pivots occur, and the required number of iterations is typically much smaller than $\binom{n+m}{m}$.

Returning to our theoretical point of view, we now wish to discuss termination as a mathematical certainty. There are several known ways to decide choices so as to ensure termination. Probably the most elegant scheme was devised by Bland [2] in 1977. The relevant definition and theorem follow. (The proof of the theorem is equally valid for the first SIMPLEX variation mentioned in connection with Definition 5.)

**Definition 6** (Bland's Smallest Subscript Rules).

(i) Determine the pivot column by choosing the negative objective entry with smallest column heading.
(ii) Break ties for minimum $\theta$-ratio by requiring the pivot to have the smallest possible row heading.

These rules are often stated as follows. Of all the variables permitted by SIMPLEX to enter the basis, choose the one with smallest subscript. Of all the variables then permitted to leave the basis, again choose the one with smallest subscript. [We note that rule (ii) is the same as Beale's second rule.]

**Theorem 9** (Bland's Termination Theorem). *SIMPLEX augmented by Bland's smallest subscript rules always terminates and never repeats a basis.*

*Proof.* Let $T_1, \ldots, T_k$ be any sequence of tableaux generated by SIMPLEX with Bland's rules. The theorem will be proved once we show that $T_1$ *and* $T_k$ *have different bases.* The latter is immediate if $T_1$ and $T_k$ have unequal corner numbers (Theorem 2). Therefore we assume that these corner numbers are equal. It then follows that *all the tableaux* $T_1, \ldots, T_k$ *have equal corner numbers* (Theorem 5).

Let us say that a variable is *active* if it changes from basic to nonbasic, or vice versa, at least once in the sequence $T_1, \ldots, T_k$. The opposite kind of variable, one that remains either basic or nonbasic throughout the entire sequence, is called *inactive*. A crucial property of an active variable is that, whenever it is basic, the constant in its row is zero. This property is ensured by our Theorem 7. Namely, since all the tableaux have equal corner numbers, they all have the same basic solution. Since an active variable is nonbasic in at least one of the tableaux, it has the value zero in this common basic solution.

The proof of the theorem is executed by studying the behavior of *the active variable, say $x_t$, with largest subscript*. Of all the active variables, $x_t$ is the one least favored by Bland's rules for a "change of status"; that is, a change from basic to nonbasic, or vice versa. As a result, we assert that $x_t$ *changes status only once*. The proof of this assertion will complete the proof of the theorem. Indeed, it will then follow that $x_t$ is basic in one of $T_1$ and $T_k$, and nonbasic in the other. Consequently, $T_1$ and $T_k$ have different bases.

Let us suppose that our assertion is false, that is, that $x_t$ changes status more than once. Then there is a tableau D somewhere in the sequence $T_1, \ldots, T_k$ with $x_t$ "departing," and another tableau E with $x_t$ "entering." These two tableaux have the following forms:

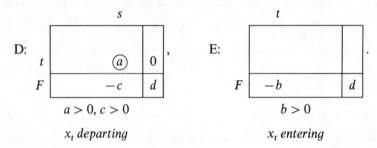

$x_t$ departing $\qquad\qquad\qquad$ $x_t$ entering

Displayed in tableau D are the subscript $t$ of the departing variable $x_t$, the subscript $s$ of the entering (active) variable $x_s$, the positive pivot $a$, the corresponding negative objective entry $-c$, the corner number $d$, the constant 0 in the row of the (active) variable $x_t$, and the symbol $F$ of the objective function. The tableau E has fewer relevant parts. The pivot is somewhere in the $x_t$ column, above the objective entry $-b$.

A specific (nonfeasible) solution of the equivalent linear systems of tableaux D and E will lead us to the desired contradiction. We define this solution, which we denote by $S$, in a now familiar way, using tableau D. Here are the relevant properties of $S$:

$$S: \begin{cases} x_s \text{ has the value 1;} \\ \text{all other nonbasic variables in D have the value 0;} \\ x_t \text{ has the value } -a; \\ \text{all active variables except } x_t \text{ have nonnegative values.} \end{cases}$$

The last statement is seen as follows. Let $x_u$ be any active variable other than $x_t$. If $x_u$ is nonbasic in D, its value in the solution $S$, by definition, is either 1 or 0. If $x_u$ is basic, we can display the situation in the following way:

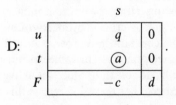

Since $x_u$ is active, $u < t$. But Bland's rules chose $a$ as pivot. Therefore the entry $q$ cannot be positive. Hence $-q$, the value of $x_u$ in the solution $S$, is nonnegative, as asserted.

Finally, we compute $F(S)$ from both D and E (Theorem 1). From D we easily obtain $F(S) = c + d$. To compute $F(S)$ from E, we consider an arbitrary objective entry $e$ other than $-b$ and the corresponding nonbasic variable, say $x_r$:

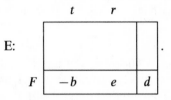

E:

Let $v$ be the value of $x_r$ in the solution $S$. Then

$$F(S) - b(-a) + ev + \cdots = d,$$

where the undisplayed terms are the same type as $ev$. We assert that $ev \geq 0$. There are two cases. If $x_r$ is active, then $r < t$. Since Bland's rules chose $x_t$ to be the entering variable, $e$ must be nonnegative. Also $v$ is nonnegative, for it is the value in $S$ of an active variable different from $x_t$. Thus $ev \geq 0$. On the other hand, if $x_r$ is inactive, it is nonbasic in every tableau, notably D. In this case, $v$ is either 1 or 0. But $x_r \neq x_s$ because $x_s$ is active. Hence $v$ and therefore $ev$ are both equal to zero.

Our contradiction is now at hand. Let $\sigma$ be the sum of all terms such as $ev$. We have shown that $\sigma \geq 0$. Replacing $F(S)$ by $c + d$ in the last equation, we obtain

$$c + d + ab + \sigma = d$$

$$c + ab + \sigma = 0.$$

The left side of the last equation is positive, and the proof is therefore complete.    □

The fact that SIMPLEX can be forced to terminate will be of great theoretical importance in future chapters. On the other hand, Theorem 9 has small practical value. In real-world applications of SIMPLEX, it is the speed and not the fact of termination that is usually the issue. Bland's method is not the fastest SIMPLEX scheme, and therefore is not often employed in computer solutions of LP problems. While on the subject of computers, we remark that a variation of SIMPLEX known as the *revised simplex method* is frequently more suitable than SIMPLEX itself for the solution of large-scale practical problems. We shall not discuss the revised simplex method further.

We conclude the chapter with a previously mentioned, now obvious theorem.

**Theorem 10.** *The objective function of an LP problem in simplex form either has a maximum value or is unbounded above. In the first case some basic solution is an OFS (more explicitly: a basic solution of a linear system equivalent to the given system of equality constraints).*

*Proof.* SIMPLEX, with Bland's rules, for instance, can be made to bring the problem to termination; either the optimality pattern or the unboundedness pattern is produced. The conclusions then follow from Theorem 3 or Theorem 4.  □

The first conclusion of Theorem 10 is a step in justifying our definition of solving an LP problem, namely, Definition 5 of Chapter 2; the final step comes in Chapter 4 when we show that the conclusion to *any* LP problem is one of the *three* outcomes described in this definition.

PROBLEMS

1. For the tableau immediately following, determine whether 0 is a feasible value of $F$.

|   | 1 | 2 |   |
|---|---|---|---|
| 3 | $-1$ | 1 | $-2$ |
| 4 | 2 | $-1$ | 5 |
| F | $-1$ | 4 | 0 |

.

   *Hint*: The general feasible solution is $(s, t, s - t - 2, -2s + t + 5)$, with all four components nonnegative. The objective row gives

$$F(s, t, s - t - 2, -2s + t + 5) = s - 4t.$$

   Therefore you need $s = 4t$ in conjunction with the four nonnegativity constraints.

2. Same as Problem 1 except that the objective entry 4 is replaced by 2.

3. (a) Pivot the tableau of Problem 1 at the entry $-1$ in the top row.
   (b) Explain the exact sense in which the given formula for $F$ and your new formula for $F$ are compatible.
   (c) Construct a proof of what you asserted in (b).

4. Suppose an LP problem has the same constraints as that of Problem 1, but that the objective function is given by $H(x_1, x_2, x_3, x_4) = \frac{1}{2}x_1 + x_2 + \frac{3}{2}x_3 + 2x_4$. Given that $H$ is to be maximized, represent this LP problem by a condensed tableau.
   *Answer*: The objective row is $H$ | 2 $-\frac{3}{2}$ | 7 | .

5. Show that if the tableau of Problem 1 is pivoted at the entry 2, the tableau

|   | 4 | 2 |   |
|---|---|---|---|
| 3 | $\frac{1}{2}$ | $\frac{1}{2}$ | $\frac{1}{2}$ |
| 1 | $\frac{1}{2}$ | $-\frac{1}{2}$ | $\frac{5}{2}$ |
| F | $\frac{1}{2}$ | $\frac{7}{2}$ | $\frac{5}{2}$ |

is obtained. From this tableau construct your own proof that max $F = F(\frac{5}{2}, 0, \frac{1}{2}, 0) = \frac{5}{2}$. You must verify that $(\frac{5}{2}, 0, \frac{1}{2}, 0)$ is a feasible solution and show that $F(s_1, s_2, s_3, s_4) \leq \frac{5}{2}$ for any feasible solution $(s_1, s_2, s_3, s_4)$.

6. For the following tableau prove without any pivoting that every feasible value of $F$ is strictly less than 5. Afterward, pivot at $-2$ and show that max $F = \frac{9}{2}$.

|   | 1 | 2 |   |
|---|---|---|---|
| 3 | $-2$ | 0 | $-1$ |
| 4 | $-4$ | 2 | 9 |
| F | 1 | 3 | 5 |

7. Solve by SIMPLEX the LP problem represented below, and show that max $F = F(\frac{17}{2}, 8, 0, 0) = \frac{19}{4}$. Then, for the purposes of Problem 8, write down the basic solution of every tableau that appears. Begin with $(0, 0, 1, 2)$ and go in order.

|   | 1 | 2 |   |
|---|---|---|---|
| 3 | 2 | $-2$ | 1 |
| 4 | 0 | $\frac{1}{4}$ | 2 |
| F | $-\frac{3}{2}$ | 1 | 0 |

8. The problem just solved could have arisen by enlargement of an LP problem in primal form with variables $x_1$ and $x_2$. Write down this problem, with $f$ denoting the objective function. Sketch the feasible region $\mathcal{R}$. Note that each basic solution generated by SIMPLEX in Problem 7 corresponds (by dropping the last two components) to a vertex of $\mathcal{R}$. Note also that consecutive basic solutions correspond to adjacent vertices. Finally, observe that the corner number of each tableau equals the value of $f$ at the corresponding vertex.

Problems 7 and 8 illustrate much of the *geometry* associated with SIMPLEX. Let us make a few preparatory remarks and then describe the general geometric situation. As mentioned before, "vertex" can be defined in any number of dimensions. Also, if $\mathcal{R}$ and $\mathcal{E}(\mathcal{R})$ are the respective feasible regions of any primal-form problem and its enlargement, then $\mathcal{R}$ and $\mathcal{E}(\mathcal{R})$ are in one-to-one correspondence "with preservation of vertices." Next, the concept of an *edge* of $\mathcal{R}$ or $\mathcal{E}(\mathcal{R})$ exists in general, and each edge either "joins two vertices" or "goes from some vertex to infinity." Two vertices joined by an edge are called *adjacent*. We are now ready: *The geometric description of SIMPLEX is a "walk" along (a subset of) the vertices* of the feasible region [either $\mathscr{R}$ or $\mathscr{E}(\mathscr{R})$]. Any two consecutive vertices in the walk are either adjacent or identical. The second case, "stepping on" the same vertex more than once, corresponds to stalling, as in Theorem 7. At each new vertex, the value of the objective function increases. The walk ends at a vertex $V$ with one of the following two properties.

(i) The objective function achieves its maximum value at $V$.
(ii) The feasible region has an edge going from $V$ to infinity, and on this edge the objective function increases without bound as the distance from $V$ increases.

(We have, of course, not included full definitions and proofs in this discussion.)

9. Solve by SIMPLEX:

|   | 1 | 2 | 3 | |
|---|---|---|---|---|
| 4 | 2 | −3 | 0 | 4 |
| 5 | 1 | 0 | −1 | 0 |
| F | −2 | 3 | 1 | 0 |

Stalling will occur on the way to optimality.
*Answer*: max $F = F(2, 0, 2, 0, 0) = 2$.

10. Solve by SIMPLEX:

|   | 1 | 2 | |
|---|---|---|---|
| 3 | −2 | 1 | 1 |
| 4 | −1 | 2 | 5 |
| 5 | 1 | −3 | 2 |
| F | 2 | −5 | 0 |

*Answer*: $F$ is unbounded above.

11. Solve by SIMPLEX:

|   | 1 | 2 | 3 | |
|---|---|---|---|---|
| 4 | 8 | 11 | −2 | 0 |
| 5 | −3 | −5 | 1 | 4 |
| F | 1 | 2 | −1 | 0 |

The number of negative objective entries will increase before optimality is reached. (Such an increase is no cause for discouragement; the best measure of progress is the amount of increase of the corner number.)
*Answer*: max $F = F(0, 8, 44, 0, 0) = 28$.

12. Solve by SIMPLEX:

|   | 1 | 2 |   |
|---|---|---|---|
| 3 | -2 | 1 | 1 |
| 4 | -3 | 2 | 5 |
| 5 | 4 | -2 | 2 |
| F | 2 | -5 | 0 |

Before optimality is reached, a certain variable will leave the basis and return again. (This is a common phenomenon.)

*Answer:* max $F = F(7, 13, 2, 0, 0) = 51$.

13. Prove that SIMPLEX never permits a variable to leave the basis and then return in the very next tableau.

14. Find the maximum of $f(x_1, x_2, x_3) = 10x_1 + 6x_2 - 8x_3$ subject to the constraints

$$5x_1 - 2x_2 + 6x_3 \le 20,$$
$$10x_1 + 4x_2 - 6x_3 \le 30, \qquad x_1, x_2, x_3 \ge 0.$$

(Remember to discard the slack variable values before stating your conclusion.)

*Answer:* max $f = f(0, 25, \frac{35}{3}) = \frac{170}{3}$.

15. Find the maximum of $f(x_1, x_2, x_3) = 2x_2 + x_3$ subject to

$$x_1 + x_2 - 2x_3 \le 7,$$
$$-3x_1 + x_2 + 2x_3 \le 3, \qquad x_1, x_2, x_3 \ge 0.$$

*Answer:* $f$ is unbounded above.

16. Find the minimum of $g(x_1, x_2) = x_1 - x_2$ subject to

$$3x_1 - x_2 \ge -1,$$
$$-6x_1 + 5x_2 \ge -6, \qquad x_1, x_2 \ge 0.$$
$$3x_1 - 2x_2 \ge -5,$$

*Answer:* $g$ is unbounded below.

17. In Problem 5 the maximum of the objective function $F$ of Problem 1 was found to be $\frac{5}{2}$. Now find the *minimum* of $F$, subject to the same constraints. Note from your answer that the corner number 0 of Problem 1 lies between the minimum and maximum values of $F$. (It can be proved that if an objective function in LP has both a minimum and a maximum value, then every number between is a feasible value of that objective function.)

*Answer:* min $F = F(3, 1, 0, 0) = -1$.

18. Solve the boat problem, stated in Problem 1 of Chapter 2.

*Answer:* Build four rowboats, 10 canoes, and 36 kayaks. The maximum monthly profit is $6,620.

19. In an application of SIMPLEX, suppose there is a tie for minimum $\theta$-ratio in the pivot column of one of the tableaux. Prove that the basic solution of the next tableau will be degenerate.

20. By reexamining the proof of Theorem 5, show that a SIMPLEX pivoting operation increases the corner number by the product of two numbers associated with the pivot column, namely,

   (i) the absolute value of the negative objective entry, and
   (ii) the minimum $\theta$-ratio.

   In light of this fact consider the following (well-known) addition to the SIM-PLEX instructions: *Select the pivot column to maximize* (i). The object of this scheme is to produce a large product of factors (i) and (ii) without the excessive computation needed to maximize this product precisely. The more complicated factor (ii) is accordingly ignored. For comparison purposes, consider any other column selection scheme that ignores (ii). (Example: Take the first negative objective entry encountered.) Presumably, then, factor (ii) has no tendency to be larger under one scheme than under the other. Therefore the product of (i) and (ii) should tend to be larger under the first scheme. Larger increments in corner numbers, in turn, usually (but not invariably) bring termination with fewer iterations. [The required number of iterations in the scheme of maximizing (i) has usually proved to be less than three times the number of equality constraints.]

   In the solution of practical LP problems, however, it is the total computing time that is paramount, not the number of iterations. For modern large-scale problems there are variations of SIMPLEX that (generally) are faster, more sophisticated, and better suited to computer implementation than any method described in this book. Reference [3] has details.

   For the small-scale, instructional LP problems in this book, there is little point in restricting the choice of negative objective entry to one of greatest absolute value. There is one exception: Beale's example depends for its success (?) on this scheme.

21. All the objective entries of a simplex tableau are positive. Prove that the basic solution of the tableau is the only OFS.

22. Show that the basic solution of the tableau below is the only OFS even though the positivity condition of Problem 21 is not present (however, see Problem 24).

|   | 3 | 4 |   |
|---|---|---|---|
| 1 | 2 | $-4$ | 6 |
| 2 | 5 | $-3$ | 0 |
| $F$ | 0 | 7 | 8 |

23. Replace the entry 5 of the preceding tableau by $-5$. Now there are infinitely many OFSs. Find all of them.
   *Answer*: $(6 - 2t, 5t, t, 0)$ with $0 \le t \le 3$.

24. If there is a zero objective entry in an "optimal" simplex tableau, and the basic solution is nondegenerate, then there are infinitely many OFSs.

*Hint*: Let the nonbasic variable associated with the zero objective entry have a small positive value.

25. Find all OFSs:

|   | 5 | 3 | 6 | 4 |   |
|---|---|---|---|---|---|
| 1 | $-1$ | $-3$ | $-2$ | 0 | 6 |
| 2 | 1 | 0 | $-4$ | 5 | 4 |
| F | $\frac{1}{2}$ | 0 | $\frac{3}{2}$ | 0 | 7 |

*Answer*: $(3s + 6, 4 - 5t, s, t, 0, 0)$ with $s \geq 0$ and $0 \leq t \leq \frac{4}{5}$.

26. Find the unique simplex tableau T with the following two properties.

(i) One SIMPLEX pivoting operation—without Beale's additional rules—takes T into Beale's tableau V.

(ii) The corner number of T is negative.

*Hint*: It follows from (i) that if V is pivoted at the same tableau position, T is obtained. It also follows that V must be pivoted at a positive entry above a *positive* objective entry, if T is to be obtained.

Next, explain how the infinite sequence

$$T, V, VI, I, \ldots, VI, I, \ldots, VI, \ldots$$

can be generated under the rules of SIMPLEX. Finally, note that the corner numbers in these tableaux are eventually all equal, as in Theorem 8, but not all equal.

27. Solve Beale's LP problem by Bland's rules. You will find that Beale's rules and Bland's rules agree on the first four choices of pivot.

28. An LP problem in primal form has nonnegative constants, more variables than $\leq$ constraints, and a unique OFS. Prove that at least one of the variables has the value zero in the OFS.

*Hint*: Any simplex tableau representing the enlarged problem has more columns than rows.

# CHAPTER 4

# Dual Tableaux and Two-Phase Algorithms

The main theoretical tool for this chapter and the next is the consideration of a "mate" for every condensed tableau. All condensed tableaux are thereby paired off, and the members of each pair are called *dual tableaux*. The fundamental property of dual tableaux, roughly stated, is that the results of pivoting both can be obtained by pivoting only one of them.

An intuitive way to think of the dual tableau is as a "mirror image." Here is an example:

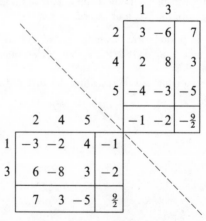

$$(1)$$

With the dotted line as a "mirror," each tableau (including row and column headings but not objective function symbols) is a "reflection" of the other. Note, however, that certain entries are the negatives of their reflections. Without this exception the fundamental property mentioned above—made precise in Theorem 1 below—would fail. The following "checkerboard" pattern indicates which members of either tableau are identical to their reflections, and which are the negatives:

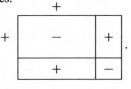

Our formal definition follows.

**Definition 1.** Two condensed tableaux of the form immediately below are called *dual tableaux*, and either is the *dual (tableau)* of the other.

| | $k_1$ | $k_2$ | $\cdots$ | $k_n$ | |
|---|---|---|---|---|---|
| $j_1$ | $\alpha_{11}$ | $\alpha_{12}$ | $\cdots$ | $\alpha_{1n}$ | $\beta_1$ |
| $j_1$ | $\alpha_{21}$ | $\alpha_{22}$ | $\cdots$ | $\alpha_{2n}$ | $\beta_2$ |
| $\vdots$ | $\vdots$ | $\vdots$ | | $\vdots$ | $\vdots$ |
| $j_m$ | $\alpha_{m1}$ | $\alpha_{m2}$ | $\cdots$ | $\alpha_{mn}$ | $\beta_m$ |
| $F$ | $\gamma_1$ | $\gamma_2$ | $\cdots$ | $\gamma_n$ | $\delta$ |

| | $j_1$ | $j_2$ | $\cdots$ | $j_m$ | |
|---|---|---|---|---|---|
| $k_1$ | $-\alpha_{11}$ | $-\alpha_{21}$ | $\cdots$ | $-\alpha_{m1}$ | $\gamma_1$ |
| $k_2$ | $-\alpha_{12}$ | $-\alpha_{22}$ | $\cdots$ | $-\alpha_{m2}$ | $\gamma_2$ |
| $\vdots$ | $\vdots$ | $\vdots$ | | $\vdots$ | $\vdots$ |
| $k_n$ | $-\alpha_{1n}$ | $-\alpha_{2n}$ | $\cdots$ | $-\alpha_{mn}$ | $\gamma_n$ |
| $H$ | $\beta_1$ | $\beta_2$ | $\cdots$ | $\beta_m$ | $-\delta$ |

$$(2)$$

The requirements are the following:

(i) The number of rows of either tableau equals the number of columns of the other.

(ii) The objective entries of either tableau, in left-to-right order, are precisely the constants of the other tableau, in top-to-bottom order. In the language of matrix theory, the matrix of objective entries of either tableau is the *transpose* of the matrix of constants of the other.

(iii) Similarly, the column headings of either tableau are the row headings of the other, again in corresponding order.

(iv) The respective corner numbers are negatives of each other.

(v) The "main bodies" of the two tableaux, that is, the matrices remaining after headings, constants, and objective rows are removed, are *negative transposes* of each other. (This means that the elements of any *row* of either matrix are the respective *negatives*, in order, of the corresponding *column* of the other.)

An immediate consequence of Definition 1 is that for any condensed tableau, there is one and only one condensed tableau that can be its dual. (Objective function symbols are excluded from consideration here.) An obvious consequence of (ii) is that if all the constants and all the objective entries of a condensed tableau are nonnegative, then the same is true of the dual tableau. Otherwise expressed, if a condensed tableau is a simplex tableau with the optimality pattern, then so is the dual tableau. The two underlying LP problems are then simultaneously solved, with OFSs and maximum feasible values on display. This simple fact will be quite useful in Chapter 5.

Next, we need a formal definition of a "pair of mirror images" in the main bodies of two dual tableaux.

**Definition 2.** With reference to the dual tableaux (2) of Definition 1, let $r$ and $s$ be any integers satisfying $1 \leq r \leq m$ and $1 \leq s \leq n$. Then the entry $\alpha_{rs}$ in row $r$ and column $s$ of the first tableau, and the entry $-\alpha_{rs}$ in row $s$ and column $r$ of the other tableau are *corresponding entries*. If $\alpha_{rs} \neq 0$, and if the two tableaux are pivoted at $\alpha_{rs}$ and $-\alpha_{rs}$, respectively, then $\alpha_{rs}$ and $-\alpha_{rs}$ are *corresponding pivots*.

Let us illustrate Definition 2 and our forthcoming Theorem 1 by means of the dual tableaux (1) above. In these tableaux we choose corresponding pivots $-2$ and 2, respectively:

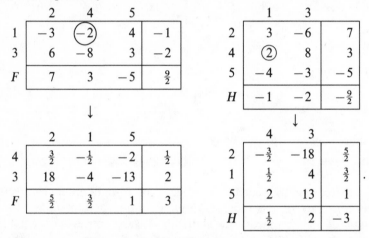

The conclusion is that the two new tableaux are again dual tableaux! Both could have been obtained by pivoting just one of the original tableaux and then writing down the dual of the result.

The last pair of dual tableaux also illustrates a comment made above: The LP problems represented by these two tableaux are both solved; the conclusions are that max $F = F(0, 0, 2, \frac{1}{2}, 0) = 3$, and max $H = H(\frac{3}{2}, \frac{5}{2}, 0, 0, 1) = -3$.

The fundamental theorem on pivoting dual tableaux is the following.

**Theorem 1.** *If dual tableaux are pivoted at corresponding entries, the two resulting tableaux are again dual tableaux.*

*Proof.* Let the dual tableaux be as in (2). The first tableau, with $\alpha_{rs}$ chosen as pivot and relevant entries displayed, is

| | $k_q$ | $k_s$ | |
|---|---|---|---|
| $j_r$ | $\alpha_{rq}$ | $\left(\alpha_{rs}\right)$ | $\beta_r$ |
| $j_i$ | $\alpha_{iq}$ | $\alpha_{is}$ | $\beta_i$ |
| | $\gamma_q$ | $\gamma_s$ | $\delta$ |

The tableau obtained by pivoting is then

|  | $k_q$ | $j_r$ |  |
|---|---|---|---|
| $k_s$ | $\dfrac{\alpha_{rq}}{\alpha_{rs}}$ | $\dfrac{1}{\alpha_{rs}}$ | $\dfrac{\beta_r}{\alpha_{rs}}$ |
| $j_i$ | $\alpha_{iq} - \dfrac{\alpha_{is}\alpha_{rq}}{\alpha_{rs}}$ | $-\dfrac{\alpha_{is}}{\alpha_{rs}}$ | $\beta_i - \dfrac{\alpha_{is}\beta_r}{\alpha_{rs}}$ |
|  | $\gamma_q - \dfrac{\alpha_{rq}\gamma_s}{\alpha_{rs}}$ | $-\dfrac{\gamma_s}{\alpha_{rs}}$ | $\delta - \dfrac{\beta_r\gamma_s}{\alpha_{rs}}$ |

The corresponding work on the dual tableau in (2) is as follows:

|  | $j_r$ | $j_i$ |  |
|---|---|---|---|
| $k_q$ | $-\alpha_{rq}$ | $-\alpha_{iq}$ | $\gamma_q$ |
| $k_s$ | $\boxed{-\alpha_{rs}}$ | $-\alpha_{is}$ | $\gamma_s$ |
|  | $\beta_r$ | $\beta_i$ | $-\delta$ |

|  | $k_s$ | $j_i$ |  |
|---|---|---|---|
| $k_q$ | $-\dfrac{\alpha_{rq}}{\alpha_{rs}}$ | $-\alpha_{iq} + \dfrac{\alpha_{is}\alpha_{rq}}{\alpha_{rs}}$ | $\gamma_q - \dfrac{\alpha_{rq}\gamma_s}{\alpha_{rs}}$ |
| $j_r$ | $-\dfrac{1}{\alpha_{rs}}$ | $\dfrac{\alpha_{is}}{\alpha_{rs}}$ | $-\dfrac{\gamma_s}{\alpha_{rs}}$ |
|  | $\dfrac{\beta_r}{\alpha_{rs}}$ | $\beta_i - \dfrac{\alpha_{is}\beta_r}{\alpha_{rs}}$ | $-\delta + \dfrac{\beta_r\gamma_s}{\alpha_{rs}}$ |

The desired conclusion is now clear.   $\square$

If we apply Theorem 1 repeatedly, we obtain the following corollary, to be useful in Chapter 5. The proof (mathematical induction on the number of pivoting operations) can be omitted.

**Corollary 1.** *If there is a pivoting sequence leading from a condensed tableau $T_1$ to a condensed tableau $T_k$, then there is also a pivoting sequence leading from the dual of $T_1$ to the dual of $T_k$.*

We are now ready for the second topic indicated in the chapter title. We shall show that any condensed tableau with one or more negative constants can be pivoted until either

(a) a tableau with no negative constants (a simplex tableau) is reached, or
(b) a tableau is produced from which it is obvious that the associated LP problem is infeasible.

Normally, our pivoting procedure ends with outcome (a), and then SIMPLEX is applied. Thus the expression *two-phase algorithm* is explained; reaching simplex form is "phase I," and SIMPLEX is "phase II." After the second phase terminates, the underlying LP problem is solved.

Before going into the details of our phase I algorithm, we note that the ability to solve LP problems representable by a condensed tableau implies the ability to solve an arbitrary LP problem. Namely, we can pass first to the primal form replacement and then to the enlarged problem. It must be mentioned, however, that for problems with a large number of equality constraints, such a procedure is computationally inferior to certain other methods (which we shall not treat). In any case, the results of this chapter will have significant theoretical value in Chapter 5.

We shall give preference to the simplest possible Phase I algorithm, deferring until the end of the chapter some refinements that can improve computational efficiency. The core of our algorithm is simply *a negative pivot in the row of a negative constant*. A couple of examples will provide illustration before we define the algorithm precisely and prove that it "works." An example of the normal, feasible case is first:

|   | 1 | 2 | 3 | |
|---|---|---|---|---|
| 4 | $\boxed{-1}$ | 2 | 4 | $-2$ |
| 5 | 3 | $-8$ | $-20$ | $-6$ |
| F | $-1$ | 3 | 7 | 0 |

$\downarrow$

|   | 4 | 2 | 3 | |
|---|---|---|---|---|
| 1 | $-1$ | $-2$ | $-4$ | 2 |
| 5 | 3 | $\boxed{-2}$ | $-8$ | $-12$ |
| F | $-1$ | 1 | 3 | 2 |

$\downarrow$

|   | 4 | 5 | 3 | |
|---|---|---|---|---|
| 1 | $-4$ | $-1$ | 4 | 14 |
| 2 | $-\frac{3}{2}$ | $-\frac{1}{2}$ | 4 | 6 |
| F | $\frac{1}{2}$ | $\frac{1}{2}$ | $-1$ | $-4$ |

The algorithm comes to a stop, and the last tableau can now be treated by SIMPLEX.

We observe that it is possible to leave objective rows out of the pivoting, and afterward to derive the final formula for $F$ by a separate computation. Specifically, $F = x_1 - 3x_2 - 7x_3 = (14 + 4x_4 + x_5 - 4x_3) - 3(6 + \frac{3}{2}x_4 + \frac{1}{2}x_5 - 4x_3) - 7x_3 = -4 - \frac{1}{2}x_4 - \frac{1}{2}x_5 + x_3$. Another remark is that we could have reached simplex form and optimality simultaneously by pivoting the second tableau at $-8$ instead of $-2$.

The next example will prove to be infeasible, so we omit objective rows:

|   | 1 | 2 | 3 |   |
|---|---|---|---|---|
| 4 | −1 | 9 | 0 | −3 |
| 5 | 5 | −46 | 1 | 12 |
| 6 | −4 | 41 | (−1) | −10 |

↓

|   | 1 | 2 | 6 |   |
|---|---|---|---|---|
| 4 | (−1) | 9 | 0 | −3 |
| 5 | 1 | −5 | 1 | 2 |
| 3 | 4 | −41 | −1 | 10 |

↓

|   | 4 | 2 | 6 |   |
|---|---|---|---|---|
| 1 | −1 | −9 | 0 | 3 |
| 5 | 1 | 4 | 1 | −1 |
| 3 | 4 | −5 | −1 | −2 |

.

The second equality constraint, $x_5 + x_4 + 4x_2 + x_6 = -1$, is obviously incompatible with the standard nonnegativity constraints. Thus the original linear system is shown to be equivalent to one in which a single equation exhibits infeasibility. We shall soon show that *any* "infeasible condensed tableau" can be transformed by our algorithm into a tableau containing such a telltale equation. First we record the simple infeasibility criterion suggested by this example. The proof of the theorem is obvious enough to omit.

**Theorem 2.** *If a condensed tableau has a negative constant with no other negative number in its row, then the LP problem represented by the tableau is infeasible.*

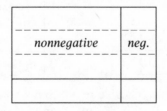

*Infeasibility Pattern*

Next, we formally define the algorithm we have illustrated. Since a negative constant and a negative pivot are required, we use the name *negative/negative algorithm,* or simply *NNA.*

**Definition 3** [Negative/Negative Algorithm (NNA)]. Applied to LP problems representable by a condensed tableau, and expressed in terms of the tableau, the algorithm NNA consists of the following steps:

   (i) Determine whether all (right-hand) constants are nonnegative. If so, stop:
       The tableau is a simplex tableau. If not, go on to step (ii).
  (ii) Determine whether there is a negative constant with no other negative
       number in its row. If so, the problem is infeasible. Stop. If not, go on to
       step (iii).
 (iii) Select a negative constant.
  (iv) Select a negative number in the row of the previous choice.
   (v) Pivot the tableau at the negative number so selected, and apply step (i)
       to the new tableau.

   As in SIMPLEX, steps (iii) and (iv) can allow several choices, and again,
as in SIMPLEX, the question of termination presents itself. The following theorem settles this question. The proof, in fact, reveals that NNA is
"SIMPLEX behind the mirror". More about this afterward.

**Theorem 3.** *The choices in NNA can be made so that an arbitrary initial
condensed tableau is brought to termination. The outcome is either the production of a simplex tableau or a tableau with an infeasibility pattern (as in Theorem
2). One way to ensure termination is to execute steps* (iii) *and* (iv) *as follows:
Select the negative constant with minimum row heading, and then select as pivot
the negative number in its row with minimum column heading.*

*Proof.* Objective rows have no effect on the course of NNA. Indeed, the two
stopping criteria and the selection of pivots involve only the linear system
portion of the condensed tableau. (Also, the computation of each succeeding
linear system depends only on the preceding one and on no prior objective
row.) It follows that it is sufficient to prove the theorem for an initial tableau
in which the objective entries are any numbers we please. We choose all zeros,
denote the initial tableau by $T_1$, and the corresponding dual tableau by $T_1^*$:

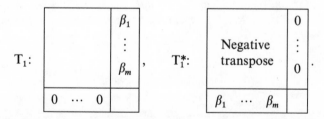

   Clearly SIMPLEX is applicable to $T_1^*$, and we have the following three
equivalences relating $T_1$ (and NNA) to $T_1^*$ (and SIMPLEX):

   (i) $T_1$ is a simplex tableau if and only if the simplex tableau $T_1^*$ has the
       optimality pattern.
  (ii) $T_1$ contains an infeasibility pattern if and only if $T_1^*$ contains an
       unboundedness pattern.
 (iii) An entry of $T_1$ is an admissible pivot under NNA if and only if the
       corresponding entry of $T_1^*$ is an admissible pivot under SIMPLEX.

Let us accept statements (i) and (ii) as obvious, and prove (iii). Suppose $\alpha_{rs}$ is an admissible NNA pivot in tableau $T_1$. Then $\alpha_{rs}$ and the constant $\beta_r$ in its row are both negative. Also, since NNA permits $T_1$ to be pivoted, there is no infeasibility pattern present. Now, $T_1^*$ contains no unboundedness pattern; the entry $-\alpha_{rs}$, corresponding to $\alpha_{rs}$ in $T_1$, is positive; it lies in the column of the negative objective entry $\beta_r$, and it has $\theta$-ratio equal to zero. Therefore SIMPLEX allows $T_1^*$ to be pivoted at $-\alpha_{rs}$. The converse implication is proved similarly.

Next, if $T_1$ is as described in either (i) or (ii), there is nothing to prove. Let us therefore suppose that both $T_1$ and $T_1^*$ require pivoting and that they are pivoted at corresponding entries in accordance with the rules of NNA and SIMPLEX, respectively. The resulting tableaux, $T_2$ and $T_2^*$, respectively, are again dual tableaux (Theorem 1). Furthermore, all the objective entries of $T_2$ and all the constants of $T_2^*$ clearly are zero. Therefore (i) through (iii) hold with $T_2$ and $T_2^*$ replacing $T_1$ and $T_1^*$, respectively. By induction, *a sequence of pivots satisfies NNA and carries $T_1$ into a tableau $T_k$ if and only if the sequence of corresponding pivots obeys SIMPLEX and carries $T_1^*$ into the dual tableau $T_k^*$.* Moreover, $T_k$ and $T_k^*$ satisfy the equivalences (i) through (iii). (We can now justifiably say that applying NNA to $T_1$ "corresponds to" applying SIMPLEX to $T_1^*$.)

To conclude, we know that there is a sequence of SIMPLEX pivots, chosen, for instance, by Bland's rules (Chapter 3, Theorem 9), carrying $T_1^*$ to a final simplex tableau. By what we have shown, this implies an NNA sequence carrying $T_1$ to termination. Finally, Bland's rules for SIMPLEX clearly correspond to the minimum heading rules for NNA stated in the present theorem. The latter rules therefore ensure termination of NNA.    □

The proof has determined the precise relationship between NNA and SIMPLEX (summarized in the next to the last paragraph). Adding the intuitive view of dual tableaux as mirror images then explains the description of NNA as "SIMPLEX behind the mirror." However, only a special case of SIMPLEX is associated with NNA, namely, SIMPLEX with all right-hand constants equal to zero. The completely general "mirror image" of SIMPLEX is an algorithm called *DUAL SIMPLEX*, discussed after the next theorem.

In applications of NNA we need not, of course, replace the objective entries by zeros; this device was employed only for purposes of the proof above. Also, we now know that an application of NNA can fail to terminate only if the corresponding application of SIMPLEX fails to terminate. Since the latter possibility is remote, we have not bothered with minimum heading rules or other precautions to ensure termination of NNA in our examples.

Combining NNA and SIMPLEX in the obvious way, we now define the two-phase algorithm NNA–SIMPLEX. The termination assertions implicit in the definition have been proved.

**Definition 4.** The algorithm NNA–SIMPLEX, for LP problems representable by a condensed tableau, is the following: Apply NNA to termination. If the outcome is infeasibility, stop. If the outcome is simplex form, apply SIMPLEX to termination.

With the help of NNA–SIMPLEX we now state our definitive theorem on solving LP problems. (Definition 5 of Chapter 2 is relevant here.) The theorem is formulated for problems representable by a condensed tableau, but as noted before, applications to general LP problems are then implied. (Some applications will appear in Chapter 5.) All the assertions in the theorem follow from Theorem 3 of this chapter and Theorems 9, 3, and 4 of Chapter 3; the results are collected here for convenient reference.

**Theorem 4.** *Every LP problem representable by a condensed tableau can be solved by pivoting, for instance under the rules of NNA–SIMPLEX. For each such problem one of the following statements holds*:

(i)  *The objective function has a maximum value.*
(ii)  *The objective function is unbounded above.*
(iii)  *The problem is infeasible.*

*Each such problem is representable by a "final" condensed tableau, obtainable by NNA–SIMPLEX, demonstrating whichever of (i), (ii), or (iii) holds. A description of such a final tableau for each case is as follows.*

(i)  *All constants and all objective entries are nonnegative. The basic solution is an OFS, and the corner number is the maximum value of the objective function.*
(ii)  *All constants are nonnegative. (Equivalently, the basic solution is feasible.) There is a negative objective entry with only nonpositive numbers in its column. A set of feasible solutions can be specified on which the objective function is unbounded above.*
(iii)  *There is a row consisting of a negative constant and all other entries nonnegative.*

We conclude the chapter by discussing some refinements of NNA. First, suppose we encounter a condensed tableau, for example,

|   | 1 | 2 | 3 |   |
|---|---|---|---|---|
| 4 | 0 | 1 | 1 | 2 |
| 5 | −1 | −1 | −2 | −3 |
| F | 5 | 2 | 8 | 0 |

with *all objective entries nonnegative*. Such a tableau could either be an initial tableau or occur in the course of pivoting. (Initial tableaux with this property arise from the diet problem and other LP problems requiring *minimization* of a function with all nonnegative coefficients.) By exercising some care in the selection of NNA pivots, we can pass this nonnegativity on to subsequent tableaux. This extra effort is usually well invested, because if a simplex tableau is reached, optimality is attained simultaneously. Thus, two phases may be reduced to one.

Instead of choosing an arbitrary (negative) pivot in the second row of the tableau above, we consider the three "modified $\theta$-ratios"

$$\frac{5}{|-1|}, \quad \frac{2}{|-1|}, \quad \frac{8}{|-2|}.$$

The middle one is the smallest, so we choose as pivot the entry $-1$ in the column of the objective entry 2. Continuing this procedure, we obtain the following sequence of tableaux:

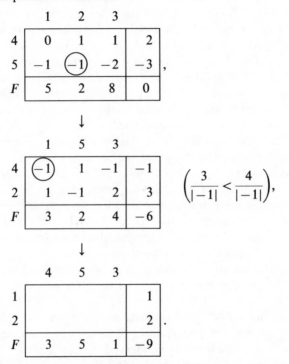

As planned, we have preserved the nonnegativity of the objective entries, and reached simplex form and optimality together.

The algorithm just employed, namely, *NNA restricted to tableaux with all nonnegative objective entries, and augmented by the "minimum modified $\theta$-ratio" requirement, is called DUAL SIMPLEX.*

To understand the operation of DUAL SIMPLEX above, we consider the dual of the original tableau, namely,

|   | 4 | 5 |   |
|---|---|---|---|
| 1 | 0 | 1 | 5 |
| 2 | $-1$ | ① | 2 |
| 3 | $-1$ | 2 | 8 |
|   | 2 | $-3$ | 0 |

This tableau can be treated by SIMPLEX. The ordinary $\theta$-ratios $\frac{5}{1}$, $\frac{2}{1}$, and $\frac{8}{2}$ correspond to the original modified $\theta$-ratios. We are thus led to the circled pivot 1 corresponding to the pivot $-1$ in the original tableau. The two tableaux obtained from these corresponding pivots are again dual tableaux, and we can again observe that a positive entry of a simplex tableau has minimum $\theta$-ratio in its column if and only if the corresponding negative entry of the dual tableau has minimum modified $\theta$-ratio in its row.

We could, in fact, prove (using reasoning like that of Theorem 3) that *any application of* SIMPLEX *completely corresponds to an application of* DUAL SIMPLEX, *and vice versa.* In such a pair of applications, corresponding pivots are employed at each stage, and the tableaux generated by one algorithm are the respective duals of those generated by the other. When SIMPLEX terminates in optimality or unboundedness, DUAL SIMPLEX correspondingly terminates in optimality or infeasibility. (That DUAL SIMPLEX cannot end in unboundedness is obvious just from the fact that the objective function has all nonpositive coefficients.)

DUAL SIMPLEX can actually be applied to any problem representable by a condensed tableau! The steps are the following: Replace the given objective entries by arbitrary positive numbers. Apply DUAL SIMPLEX to termination. If infeasibility is the outcome, stop. If a simplex tableau is reached, compute the original objective function in terms of the nonbasic variables of this simplex tableau. (This technique was illustrated earlier in an NNA example.) Finally, insert the objective entries so obtained into the simplex tableau in place of the nonnegative entries already there. Phase II can now commence. The author suspects that such phase I algorithms are likely to terminate faster (in large-scale problems) than NNA with randomly made choices.

The final variation of NNA to be discussed is the addition of a third stopping instruction. A slight generalization of the unboundedness pattern for simplex tableaux is applicable to any condensed tableau. The presence of the generalized pattern implies that the underlying LP problem is feasible and the objective function is unbounded above. Since the pattern can occur before NNA produces a simplex tableau, there exists the possibility of eliminating some computation. Unaware of the pattern in a given example, we would have to finish both phases of NNA–SIMPLEX before reaching the unboundedness conclusion. (See Problem 6 at the end of the chapter.)

Before being more explicit, we note from the simple example

|   | 1 | 4 |   |
|---|---|---|---|
| 2 | 0 | 3 | $-7$ |
| 3 | $-2$ | $-5$ | 2 |
| 5 | $-4$ | 9 | $-20$ |
| F | $-3$ | 4 | $-6$ |

that the usual SIMPLEX unboundedness pattern, present in the first column, will not suffice. Indeed, the LP problem here is infeasible. (Clear from the first row.)

Let us form a new example by interchanging the 0 and $-2$ in the first column:

|   | 1 | 4 |   |
|---|---|---|---|
| 2 | $-2$ | 3 | $-7$ |
| 3 | 0 | $-5$ | 2 |
| 5 | $-4$ | 9 | $-20$ |
| $F$ | $-3$ | 4 | $-6$ |

The 5-tuple $(t, 2t - 7, 2, 0, 4t - 20)$, generated from the equality constraints by setting $x_1 = t$ and $x_4 = 0$, is a feasible solution for any $t \geq 5$. Since $F(t, 2t - 7, 2, 0, 4t - 20) = 3t - 6$, it is clear that $F$ is unbounded on the subset $\{(t, 2t - 7, 2, 0, 4t - 20): t \geq 5\}$ of the feasible region.

The general theorem follows.

**Theorem 5** (Generalized Unboundedness Theorem). *If a condensed tableau has a negative objective entry with no positive entry in its column, and if, in addition, there is no zero in this column with a negative constant in its row, then the LP problem represented by the tableau is feasible, and the objective function is unbounded above.*

*Proof.* (Using notation and ideas of Theorem 4 of Chapter 3.) The hypotheses imply a tableau of the form

|   | $k$ |   |
|---|---|---|
| | $-\alpha_1$ | $\beta_1$ |
| | $\vdots$ | $\vdots$ |
| | $-\alpha_m$ | $\beta_m$ |
| $F$ | $-c$ | $d$ |

where the following conditions hold:

(i)  $c > 0$.
(ii)  $\alpha_1, \ldots, \alpha_m \geq 0$.
(iii)  For each $i$ $(i = 1, 2, \ldots, m)$ it is not the case that $\alpha_i = 0$ and $\beta_i < 0$.

Setting $x_k = t$ and all other nonbasic variables equal to zero, we obtain from the equality constraints the values $\alpha_1 t + \beta_1, \ldots, \alpha_m t + \beta_m$ for the basic variables. We assert that for any $i$, $\alpha_i t + \beta_i \geq 0$ for $t$ sufficiently large. Indeed, if $\beta_i \geq 0$, (ii) implies that $\alpha_i t + \beta_i \geq 0$ for all $t \geq 0$. On the other hand, if $\beta_i < 0$, then (ii) and (iii) give $\alpha_i > 0$. Therefore $\alpha_i t + \beta_i \geq 0$ for $t \geq |\beta_i|/\alpha_i$. It now follows that for $t$ sufficiently large, the values of *all* the variables are non-negative. The value of $F$ at the feasible solution so constructed is $ct + d$. By (i) the desired conclusion is now evident. $\square$

Armed with the results of this chapter, particularly Theorems 1 and 4, we are now well perepared to discuss *dual LP problems* in Chapter 5.

## PROBLEMS

1. Suppose (just for this problem) that "dual tableaux" are (incorrectly) defined simply to be transposes of each other, without the "checkerboard pattern" of the correct definition. Show that pivoting such dual tableaux at corresponding entries need *not* produce dual tableaux.

2. The system

|   | 1 | 2 | 3 |   |
|---|---|---|---|---|
| 4 | −1 | 9 | 0 | −3 |
| 5 | 5 | −46 | 1 | 12 |
| 6 | −4 | 41 | −1 | −10 |

in the text was shown to be incompatible with the usual nonnegativity constraints. Give another demonstration by pivoting first in row 1, column 1. Make use of both demonstrations to prove that any *two* of the three equations *are* consistent with the nonnegativity constraints.

3. Explain why the original result concerning the system above is equivalent to the statement that the following inequalities cannot be simultaneously satisfied:

$$\left\{ \begin{array}{l} -x_1 + 9x_2 \leq -3, \\ 5x_1 - 46x_2 + x_3 \leq 12, \qquad x_1, x_2, x_3 \geq 0. \\ -4x_1 + 41x_2 - x_3 \leq -10, \end{array} \right.$$

4. Solve by NNA–SIMPLEX:

|   | 1 | 2 | 3 | 4 |   |
|---|---|---|---|---|---|
| 5 | −10 | 4 | −7 | −14 | 5 |
| 6 | 2 | −1 | 1 | 3 | −2 |
| F | 26 | −10 | 25 | 40 | 0 |

*Answer*: max $F = F(\frac{3}{2}, 5, 0, 0, 0, 0) = 11$.

5. Consider the following two almost identical tableaux.

|   | 1 | 2 | 3 |   |
|---|---|---|---|---|
| 4 | −1 | 1 | −2 | 8 |
| 5 | 0 | −2 | 3 | 5 |
| 6 | 0 | 1 | −1 | −2 |
| F | −1 | 3 | 4 | −9 |

|   | 1 | 2 | 3 |   |
|---|---|---|---|---|
| 4 | −1 | 1 | −2 | 8 |
| 5 | 0 | −2 | 3 | 7 |
| 6 | 0 | 1 | −1 | −2 |
| F | −1 | 3 | 4 | −9 |

Each has a negative objective entry with no positive number in its column. Theorem 5 is not applicable to either one. Apply NNA–SIMPLEX to both and show that the LP problems represented by these two tableaux have different outcomes.

6. Solve the following problem, first with the aid of Theorem 5, then without:

|   | 1 | 2 |   |
|---|---|---|---|
| 3 | −1 | 3 | −1 |
| 4 | 0 | −2 | −2 |
| 5 | −4 | 9 | −6 |
| F | −3 | 4 | 0 |

7. In Chapter 2, for the problem: minimize

$$g(x_1, x_2, x_3) = 2x_1 + x_2 + 3x_3,$$

$$-3x_1 + 2x_2 + 4x_3 \geq 20, \qquad\qquad x_1, x_2, x_3 \geq 0,$$

$$x_1 + x_2 + x_3 = 7,$$

it was suggested that min $g = g(0, 4, 3) = 13$. Use your current knowledge to solve this problem, and show that this information is correct.

8. The diet problem with feeds, costs, nutrients, and MDRs given by the chart

|   | $F_1$ | $F_2$ | MDR |
|---|---|---|---|
| $N_1$ | 5 | 1 | 11 |
| $N_2$ | 2 | 1 | 8 |
| $N_3$ | 1 | 2 | 7 |
| Cents/pound | 40 | 30 | |

was treated in Problems 2 through 5 of Chapter 2. Solve it now by DUAL SIMPLEX.

*Answer*: 3 pounds of $F_1$ and 2 pounds of $F_2$ to each farm animal.

9. Solve the diet problem specified as follows:

|   | $F_1$ | $F_2$ | $F_3$ | MDR |
|---|---|---|---|---|
| $N_1$ | 2 | 5 | 4 | 8 |
| $N_2$ | 3 | 1 | 6 | 7 |
| $N_3$ | 4 | 3 | 1 | 9 |
| Cents/pound | 12 | 15 | 4 | |

*Answer*: 2 pounds of $F_1$, no $F_2$, and 1 pound of $F_3$.

# CHAPTER 5

# Dual LP Problems

Perhaps the reader can guess the upcoming relationship between *dual LP problems* and dual condensed tableaux. In any case we shall define dual LP problems independently and make contact with dual tableaux afterward. The ultimate point (roughly stated) is that solving an LP problem actually solves *two* LP problems. The principal ideas and results of this chapter (and the next one as well) have origins in the work of John von Neumann (1903–1957).

To motivate the definition of dual LP problems, we again consider the production problem of Chapter 2. The theme of this problem is the generation of products $P_j$ ($j = 1, \ldots, n$) from resources $R_i$ ($i = 1, \ldots, m$). As before, we let

$b_i = $ the number of available units of $R_i$;

$c_j = $ the net profit, in dollars, resulting from the production of one unit of $P_j$;

$a_{ij} = $ the number of units of $R_i$ required in the production of one unit of $P_j$; and

$x_j = $ the number of units of $P_j$ to be produced.

The production problem, now designated by $\mathscr{P}$, is precisely the following:

$$\mathscr{P}: \begin{cases} \text{Maximize} \quad f(x_1, \ldots, x_n) = \sum_{j=1}^{n} c_j x_j \\[2mm] \text{subject to} \quad \sum_{j=1}^{n} a_{ij} x_j \leq b_i, \qquad i = 1, \ldots, m, \\[2mm] \qquad\qquad\qquad x_j \geq 0, \qquad j = 1, \ldots, n. \end{cases}$$

Suppose now that an entrepreneur offers to buy out the manufacturer's resources, and the two attempt to agree on a value for a unit of each resource. We let $y_{n+i}$ ($i = 1, \ldots, m$) denote the number of dollars to be paid per unit of

$R_i$. (The notation $y_{n+1}, \ldots, y_{n+m}$ will prove to be very convenient throughout the chapter; the symbols $y_1, \ldots, y_n$ are reserved for another purpose.)

The manufacturer argues as follows: "For each $j$, my net profit is $c_j$ dollars per unit of $P_j$ produced. Therefore $y_{n+i}$ ($i = 1, \ldots, m$) should be such that I receive no less than $c_j$ dollars for the resources going into the production of one unit of $P_j$. These resources amount to $a_{ij}$ units of $R_i$ for every $i$. At $y_{n+i}$ dollars per unit of $R_i$, my revenue from the sale of these resources would be $\sum_{i=1}^{m} a_{ij} y_{n+i}$. Therefore the inequality $\sum_{i=1}^{m} a_{ij} y_{n+i} \geq c_j$ should hold for every $j$."

We note in passing that the inequalities desired by the manufacturer imply that $\sum_{j=1}^{n} (\sum_{i=1}^{m} a_{ij} y_{n+i}) x_j \geq \sum_{j=1}^{n} c_j x_j$. The interpretation of this inequality is that the sales revenue from the resources going into *any* production schedule ($x_j$ units of $P_j$ for each $j$) is greater than or equal to the net profit resulting from that production schedule.

Let us suppose that the entrepreneur accepts the manufacturer's conditions. Then, since the price to be paid for all the resources is $\sum_{i=1}^{m} b_i y_{n+i}$, the entrepreneur would like to solve the following LP problem. The symbol $\mathscr{P}^*$ will be convenient.

$$\mathscr{P}^*: \quad \begin{cases} \text{Minimize} \quad g(y_{n+1}, \ldots, y_{n+m}) = \sum_{i=1}^{m} b_i y_{n+i} \\ \text{subject to} \quad \sum_{i=1}^{m} a_{ij} y_{n+i} \geq c_j, \qquad j = 1, \ldots, n, \\ \qquad\qquad\qquad\quad y_{n+i} \geq 0, \qquad i = 1, \ldots, m. \end{cases}$$

We shall return to the production and entrepreneur's problems later in the chapter. For now, these problems serve as motivation for Definition 1 below of dual LP problems. In the definition we refer to the *form* of $\mathscr{P}$ and $\mathscr{P}^*$, but not necessarily to products and resources. The numbers $a_{ij}$, $b_i$, and $c_j$ need not be nonnegative, and $\mathscr{P}$ is then the general LP problem in primal form (Chapter 2, Definition 1).

**Definition 1.** Two LP problems in the form of $\mathscr{P}$ and $\mathscr{P}^*$ above are called *dual LP problems*. Also, $\mathscr{P}$ is called the *primal problem* and $\mathscr{P}^*$ the *dual problem*.

This definition is not as not as general as possible, but it is quite substantial and useful. A generalization is indicated later.

Some observations will help us construct specific pairs of dual problems. The "expanded forms" of $\mathscr{P}$ and $\mathscr{P}^*$, respectively, are the following:

$$\mathscr{P}: \quad \begin{cases} \text{Maximize} \quad f(x_1, \ldots, x_n) = c_1 x_1 + \cdots + c_n x_n \\ \text{subject to} \quad a_{11} x_1 + a_{12} x_2 + \cdots + a_{1n} x_n \leq b_1, \\ \qquad\qquad\quad a_{21} x_1 + a_{22} x_2 + \cdots + a_{2n} x_n \leq b_2, \\ \qquad\qquad\quad \vdots \qquad \vdots \qquad \vdots \qquad \vdots \qquad \vdots \\ \qquad\qquad\quad a_{m1} x_1 + a_{m2} x_2 + \cdots + a_{mn} x_n \leq b_m, \end{cases} \quad x_1, \ldots, x_n \geq 0.$$

$$\mathscr{P}^*: \begin{cases} \text{Minimize } g(y_{n+1}, \ldots, y_{n+m}) = b_1 y_{n+1} + \cdots + b_m y_{n+m} \\ \text{subject to } a_{11} y_{n+1} + a_{21} y_{n+2} + \cdots + a_{m1} y_{n+m} \geq c_1, \\ \qquad\qquad a_{12} y_{n+1} + a_{22} y_{n+2} + \cdots + a_{m2} y_{n+m} \geq c_2, \quad y_{n+1}, \ldots, y_{n+m} \geq 0. \\ \qquad\qquad \vdots \qquad\quad \vdots \qquad\quad \vdots \qquad\quad \vdots \qquad\quad \vdots \\ \qquad\qquad a_{1n} y_{n+1} + a_{2n} y_{n+2} + \cdots + a_{mn} y_{n+m} \geq c_n, \end{cases}$$

Thus, the "constraint coefficient matrices" of $\mathscr{P}$ and $\mathscr{P}^*$, respectively, are transposes of each other. In particular, the number of constraints (excluding nonnegativity constraints) in either problem equals the number of variables in the other. Finally, the (right-hand) constants of either problem are the objective function coefficients of the other.

Let us now apply Definition 1 and the subsequent remarks to write down a specific pair of dual problems, denoted $\mathscr{P}_0$ and $\mathscr{P}_0^*$:

$$\mathscr{P}_0: \begin{cases} \text{Maximize } f(x_1, x_2, x_3) = -3x_1 + x_2 - 2x_3 \\ \qquad -x_1 + 2x_2 + 4x_3 \leq \quad 8, \qquad\qquad x_1, x_2, x_3 \geq 0. \\ \qquad 6x_1 - \quad x_2 - 5x_3 \leq -9, \end{cases}$$

$$\mathscr{P}_0^*: \begin{cases} \text{Minimize } g(y_4, y_5) = 8y_4 - 9y_5, \\ \qquad -y_4 + 6y_5 \geq -3, \\ \qquad 2y_4 - \quad y_5 \geq \quad 1, \qquad\qquad y_4, y_5 \geq 0. \\ \qquad 4y_4 - 5y_5 \geq -2, \end{cases}$$

The reader should study and fully understand the joint structure of these two problems before continuing.

We can now justify the "high-subscript" notation chosen for the dual LP problem, first for the example just given and then in general. Let us denote the enlargement of problem $\mathscr{P}_0$ by $\mathscr{E}(\mathscr{P}_0)$. With slack variables $x_4$ and $x_5$, and objective function $F$, $\mathscr{E}(\mathscr{P}_0)$ and its tableau representation are the following:

$$\mathscr{E}(\mathscr{P}_0): \begin{cases} \text{Maximize } F(x_1, \ldots, x_5) = -3x_1 + x_2 - 2x_3, \\ \qquad x_4 - \quad x_1 + 2x_2 + 4x_3 = \quad 8, \qquad\qquad x_1, \ldots, x_5 \geq 0; \\ \qquad x_5 + 6x_1 - \quad x_2 - 5x_3 = -9, \end{cases}$$

|   | 1 | 2 | 3 |   |
|---|---|---|---|---|
| 4 | −1 | 2 | 4 | 8 |
| 5 | 6 | −1 | −5 | −9 |
| F | 3 | −1 | 2 | 0 |

Turning next to $\mathcal{P}_0^*$, we require first its primal form replacement, namely,

$$\left\{ \begin{array}{l} \text{Maximize} \quad h(y_4, y_5) = -g(y_4, y_5) = -8y_4 + 9y_5, \\[4pt] \qquad\quad y_4 - 6y_5 \leq \quad 3, \\[4pt] \qquad -2y_4 + \ y_5 \leq -1, \\[4pt] \qquad -4y_4 + 5y_5 \leq \quad 2, \end{array} \right. \qquad y_4, y_5 \geq 0.$$

Now comes the point. We have saved the symbols $y_1$, $y_2$, and $y_3$ to denote the slack variables in the enlargement of the last problem. This enlargement, denoted $\mathscr{E}(\mathcal{P}_0^*)$, and the corresponding tableau then appear as follows:

$$\mathscr{E}(\mathcal{P}_0^*)\colon \left\{ \begin{array}{l} \text{Maximize} \quad H(y_1, \ldots, y_5) = -8y_4 + 9y_5, \\[4pt] \qquad y_1 + \ y_4 - 6y_5 = \quad 3, \\[4pt] \qquad y_2 - 2y_4 + \ y_5 = -1, \\[4pt] \qquad y_3 - 4y_4 + 5y_5 = \quad 2, \end{array} \right. \qquad y_1, \ldots, y_5 \geq 0;$$

|   | 4 | 5 |   |
|---|---|---|---|
| 1 | 1 | −6 | 3 |
| 2 | −2 | 1 | −1 |
| 3 | −4 | 5 | 2 |
| H | 8 | −9 | 0 |

The conclusion is that the tableaux representing $\mathscr{E}(\mathcal{P}_0)$ and $\mathscr{E}(\mathcal{P}_0^*)$ are dual tableaux! It is worth noting in particular that the decision variable subscripts of either problem are the slack variable subscripts of the other.

We shall shortly prove in general what has just been illustrated: *The enlargements of dual LP problems are represented by dual tableaux.* This fact, together with Theorem 1 of Chapter 4, will enable us to work on both of two dual problems simultaneously and to present a clear proof of the famous duality theorem.

Before continuing with the main development, we discuss a question of symmetry. Technically, the duality relation for condensed tableaux is both symmetric and one to one, in a word, *involutory.* Having noted the close connection between dual tableaux and dual LP problems, we therefore can expect some symmetry in the relationship between a primal and dual LP problem, symmetry not immediately obvious from Definition 1. In Problem 3, the reader is asked to confirm this expectation by executing the following instructions:

(i) Rewrite $\mathcal{P}^*$ without "high-subscript" notation; that is, with variables $y_1, \ldots, y_m$.

(ii) Pass to the primal form replacement of $\mathcal{P}^*$, so rewritten.

(iii) With the latter as primal problem, construct the dual problem as in Definition 1, but with variables, say, $z_1, \ldots, z_n$.

(iv) Again pass to the primal-form replacement.

 (v) Observe that the result is problem $\mathscr{P}$, except for the notation for the variables.

As a result of this exercise it is often stated that the dual of $\mathscr{P}^*$ is $\mathscr{P}$, or "the dual of the dual is the primal." These statements assume that every LP problem is identified with its primal form replacement. This identification plus our Definition 1 can be used to define the dual of an arbitrary LP problem. We shall make no further reference to the material in this paragraph.

We now formally define $\mathscr{E}(\mathscr{P})$ and $\mathscr{E}(\mathscr{P}^*)$, and prove the announced theorem relating dual problems and dual tableaux. The full details of the definition appear in the theorem.

**Definition 2.** Let the dual LP problems $\mathscr{P}$ and $\mathscr{P}^*$ be as in Definition 1. Then the enlargement of $\mathscr{P}$, with slack variables $x_{n+1}, \ldots, x_{n+m}$, is denoted $\mathscr{E}(\mathscr{P})$. Similarly, the enlargement of the primal form replacement of $\mathscr{P}^*$, with slack variables $y_1, \ldots, y_n$, is denoted $\mathscr{E}(\mathscr{P}^*)$.

**Theorem 1.** $\mathscr{E}(\mathscr{P})$ and $\mathscr{E}(\mathscr{P}^*)$ are representable by dual tableaux.

*Proof.* The problem $\mathscr{E}(\mathscr{P})$, with $F$ denoting the objective function, is the following:

$$\mathscr{E}(\mathscr{P}): \quad \begin{cases} \text{Maximize} \quad F(x_1, \ldots, x_{n+m}) = \sum_{j=1}^{n} c_j x_j \\[2ex] \text{subject to} \quad x_{n+i} + \sum_{j=1}^{n} a_{ij} x_j = b_i, \quad i = 1, \ldots, m, \\[2ex] \qquad\qquad\qquad\qquad x_k \geq 0, \qquad k = 1, \ldots, n + m. \end{cases}$$

Hence $\mathscr{E}(\mathscr{P})$ is represented by the tableau

|       | 1        | 2        | $\cdots$ | $n$      |          |
|-------|----------|----------|----------|----------|----------|
| $n+1$ | $a_{11}$ | $a_{12}$ | $\cdots$ | $a_{1n}$ | $b_1$    |
| $n+2$ | $a_{21}$ | $a_{22}$ | $\cdots$ | $a_{2n}$ | $b_2$    |
| $\vdots$ | $\vdots$ | $\vdots$ |       | $\vdots$ | $\vdots$ |
| $n+m$ | $a_{m1}$ | $a_{m2}$ | $\cdots$ | $a_{mn}$ | $b_m$    |
| $F$   | $-c_1$   | $-c_2$   | $\cdots$ | $-c_n$   | $0$      |

Now for the dual problem. The primal form replacement of $\mathscr{P}^*$ is the problem of

$$\begin{cases} \text{maximizing} \quad h(y_{n+1}, \ldots, y_{n+m}) = \sum_{i=1}^{m} (-b_i)y_{n+i} \\ \text{subject to} \quad \sum_{i=1}^{m} (-a_{ij})y_{n+i} \leq -c_j, \quad j = 1, \ldots, n, \\ \qquad\qquad\qquad y_{n+i} \geq 0, \qquad i = 1, \ldots, m. \end{cases}$$

Therefore $\mathscr{E}(\mathscr{P}^*)$, with objective function $H$, is given as follows:

$$\mathscr{E}(\text{P}^*): \begin{cases} \text{Maximize} \quad H(y_1, \ldots, y_{n+m}) = \sum_{i=1}^{m} (-b_i)y_{n+i} \\ \text{subject to} \quad y_j + \sum_{i=1}^{m} (-a_{ij})y_{n+i} = -c_j, \qquad j = 1, \ldots, n, \\ \qquad\qquad\qquad y_k \geq 0, \qquad k = 1, \ldots, n + m. \end{cases}$$

The tableau representation is

|  | $n + 1$ | $n + 2$ | $\cdots$ | $n + m$ | |
|---|---|---|---|---|---|
| 1 | $-a_{11}$ | $-a_{21}$ | $\cdots$ | $-a_{m1}$ | $-c_1$ |
| 2 | $-a_{12}$ | $-a_{22}$ | $\cdots$ | $-a_{m2}$ | $-c_2$ |
| $\vdots$ | $\vdots$ | $\vdots$ | | $\vdots$ | $\vdots$ |
| $n$ | $-a_{1n}$ | $-a_{2n}$ | | $-a_{mn}$ | $-c_n$ |
| $H$ | $b_1$ | $b_2$ | $\cdots$ | $b_m$ | $0$ |

,

and this is the dual of the previous tableau.     □

Next, we illustrate how a pair of dual problems can be solved by solving only one of them. The problems are $\mathscr{P}_0$ and $\mathscr{P}_0^*$, discussed earlier. We solve $\mathscr{P}_0^*$ by applying NNA–SIMPLEX to $\mathscr{E}(\mathscr{P}_0^*)$:

|  | | 4 | 5 | |
|---|---|---|---|---|
| | 1 | 1 | $-6$ | $3$ |
| Initial Tableau of $\mathscr{E}(\mathscr{P}_0^*)$: | 2 | $-2$ | $1$ | $-1$ |
| | 3 | $-4$ | $5$ | $2$ |
| | $H$ | $8$ | $-9$ | $0$ |

↓

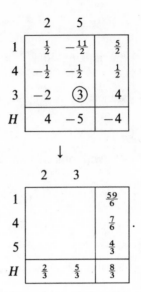

$$
\begin{array}{c|ccc}
 & 2 & 5 & \\
\hline
1 & \frac{1}{2} & -\frac{11}{2} & \frac{5}{2} \\
4 & -\frac{1}{2} & -\frac{1}{2} & \frac{1}{2} \\
3 & -2 & ③ & 4 \\
H & 4 & -5 & -4
\end{array}
$$

↓

Final tableau of $\mathscr{E}(\mathscr{P}_0^*)$:

$$
\begin{array}{c|ccc}
 & 2 & 3 & \\
\hline
1 & & & \frac{59}{6} \\
4 & & & \frac{7}{6} \\
5 & & & \frac{4}{3} \\
H & \frac{2}{3} & \frac{5}{3} & \frac{8}{3}
\end{array}
$$

From the last tableau we conclude first that max $H = H(\frac{59}{6}, 0, 0, \frac{7}{6}, \frac{4}{3}) = \frac{8}{3}$. Next, since $y_4$ and $y_5$ are the decision variables of $\mathscr{E}(\mathscr{P}_0^*)$, max $h = h(\frac{7}{6}, \frac{4}{3}) = \frac{8}{3}$. (Theorem 1 of Chapter 2 is relevant here.) Finally, since $g$ was the original objective function of $\mathscr{P}_0^*$ with $h = -g$, we conclude that min $g = g(\frac{7}{6}, \frac{4}{3}) = -\frac{8}{3}$. Thus $\mathscr{P}_0^*$ is solved.

Now, the key to solving $\mathscr{P}_0$ with no additional computation is simply that *the dual of the last written tableau represents* $\mathscr{E}(\mathscr{P}_0)$. Indeed, the pivoting sequence above, taking the first tableau into the last, implies a pivoting sequence taking the dual of the first tableau into the dual of the last (Theorem 1 and Corollary 1 of Chapter 4). But we have already seen that the dual of the first tableau represents $\mathscr{E}(\mathscr{P}_0)$. Hence so does the dual of the last, namely,

Final Tableau of $\mathscr{E}(\mathscr{P}_0)$:

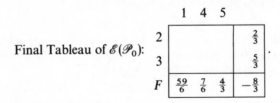

$$
\begin{array}{c|ccc|c}
 & 1 & 4 & 5 & \\
\hline
2 & & & & \frac{2}{3} \\
3 & & & & \frac{5}{3} \\
\hline
F & \frac{59}{6} & \frac{7}{6} & \frac{4}{3} & -\frac{8}{3}
\end{array}
$$

Thus, max $F = F(0, \frac{2}{3}, \frac{5}{3}, 0, 0) = -\frac{8}{3}$. Finally, since the variables of the problem $\mathscr{P}_0$ are $x_1, x_2, x_3$, our conclusion about $\mathscr{P}_0$ is that max $f = f(0, \frac{2}{3}, \frac{5}{3}) = -\frac{8}{3}$. Let us also note the important $\mathscr{P}_0/\mathscr{P}_0^*$ joint result that max $f = $ min $g$.

We could even have saved the labor of writing down the last tableau. We have read off that tableau an OFS of the original problem $\mathscr{P}_0$ by the following familiar rules: If a subscript 1, 2, or 3 of a variable $x_1, x_2,$ or $x_3$ is on the side of the tableau, the value of that variable in the OFS is the constant in the row of the subscript; if the subscript is along the top of the tableau, the value of that variable is zero. The result was $(0, \frac{2}{3}, \frac{5}{3})$. We could have obtained this OFS *from the final tableau of* $\mathscr{E}(\mathscr{P}_0^*)$ by "reversing" these rules: For each subscript 1, 2, or 3 along the top, the value of the corresponding variable $x_1, x_2$, or $x_3$ is the objective entry directly under that subscript; for each subscript along the side, the value is zero. The result is again $(0, \frac{2}{3}, \frac{5}{3})$.

Our discussion (not including the last paragraph) suggests the validity of the next theorem. Called the duality theorem, it is the principal result of this chapter, and perhaps of linear programming. The proof is now easy.

**Theorem 2** (Duality Theorem). *Let either problem* $\mathscr{P}$ *or* $\mathscr{P}^*$ *have an OFS. Then so does the other, and* max $f$ = min $g$.

*Proof.* Since either $\mathscr{P}$ or $\mathscr{P}^*$ has an OFS, the same is true of either $\mathscr{E}(\mathscr{P})$ or $\mathscr{E}(\mathscr{P}^*)$ (Theorem 1, Chapter 2). These two enlarged problems are representable by dual tableaux (Theorem 1, this chapter). By Theorem 4 of Chapter 4 there is a pivoting sequence taking one of these tableaux into a simplex tableau with the optimality pattern. The dual of this final tableau represents the other enlarged problem (Corollary 1, Chapter 4). This dual tableau, of course, is also a simplex tableau with the optimality pattern. Thus, both $\mathscr{E}(\mathscr{P})$ and $\mathscr{E}(\mathscr{P}^*)$ have OFSs. The same is then true for both $\mathscr{P}$ and $\mathscr{P}^*$. Finally, the corner numbers of the two final tableaux are negatives of each other. Therefore, with the notation of Theorem 1, max $F$ = $-$max $H$ and max $f$ = $-$max $h$ = min $g$, as required. ☐

Several remarks are of interest at this point.

(i) As suggested by the example before the theorem, OFSs of *both* $\mathscr{P}$ and $\mathscr{P}^*$ can be read off the final tableau of *either* $\mathscr{E}(\mathscr{P})$ or $\mathscr{E}(\mathscr{P}^*)$. Let us illustrate once more. Suppose the tableau

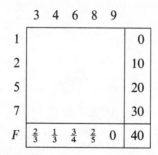

represents $\mathscr{E}(\mathscr{P})$, for some primal problem $\mathscr{P}$. (The main body of the tableau is irrelevant to our discussion.) Then $x_1, \ldots, x_5$ are decision variables and $x_6, \ldots, x_9$ are slack variables. Therefore $(0, 10, 0, 0, 20)$ is an OFS of $\mathscr{P}$. The variables of the problem $\mathscr{P}^*$ are $y_6, \ldots, y_9$, the subscripts being the same as those of the slack variables $x_6, \ldots, x_9$. By the "reversal" of the usual method of reading off the basic solution of a condensed tableau, we obtain the values $y_6 = \frac{3}{4}$, $y_7 = 0$, $y_8 = \frac{2}{5}$, and $y_9 = 0$. Hence $(\frac{3}{4}, 0, \frac{2}{5}, 0)$ is an OFS of $\mathscr{P}^*$. Of course max $f$ = min $g$ = 40.

(ii) The conclusion max $f$ = min $g$ of the duality theorem implies the apparently weaker conclusion that every feasible value of $f$ is less than or equal to every feasible value of $g$. At present these conclusions are known only under the assumption that either $\mathscr{P}$ or $\mathscr{P}*$ has an OFS. Soon we shall reach the same two conclusions, in reverse order, whenever $\mathscr{P}$ and $\mathscr{P}*$ are both feasible. We shall also see that either one or both of $\mathscr{P}$ and $\mathscr{P}*$ can be infeasible.

(iii) Applied to the production and entrepreneur's LP problems discussed earlier, the equation max $f$ = min $g$ states the following: The largest profit to be made by converting a set of resources into products is equal to the smallest price that can be paid for the set of resources while satisfying the owner's demands (appearing as constraints in problem $\mathscr{P}*$).

The following lemma will lead to further interesting and important results. In the lemma and elsewhere the notation $(t_{n+1}, \ldots, t_{n+m})$ is used for a feasible solution of the problem $\mathscr{P}*$. This high-subscript notation is consistent with that employed for the variables $y_{n+1}, \ldots, y_{n+m}$.

**Lemma 1** (Primal–Dual Identity). *Let $(s_1, \ldots, s_n)$ and $(t_{n+1}, \ldots, t_{n+m})$ be arbitrary feasible solutions of $\mathscr{P}$ and $\mathscr{P}*$, respectively. Let $(s_1, \ldots, s_{n+m})$ and $(t_1, \ldots, t_{n+m})$ be the corresponding feasible solutions of the enlarged problems $\mathscr{E}(\mathscr{P})$ and $\mathscr{E}(\mathscr{P}*)$. Then*

$$\sum_{k=1}^{n+m} s_k t_k = g(t_{n+1}, \ldots, t_{n+m}) - f(s_1, \ldots, s_n).$$

*Proof.* The numbers $s_{n+1}, \ldots, s_{n+m}$ and $t_1, \ldots, t_n$ are values of various slack variables. Precisely, from the formulations of $\mathscr{E}(\mathscr{P})$ and $\mathscr{E}(\mathscr{P}*)$ appearing in Theorem 1, we have the equations

$$s_{n+i} = b_i - \sum_{j=1}^{n} a_{ij} s_j, \qquad i = 1, \ldots, m,$$

$$t_j = \sum_{i=1}^{m} a_{ij} t_{n+i} - c_j, \qquad j = 1, \ldots, n.$$

The rest is a computation making use of these expressions:

$$\sum_{k=1}^{n+m} s_k t_k = \sum_{j=1}^{n} s_j t_j + \sum_{i=1}^{m} s_{n+i} t_{n+i}$$

$$= \sum_{j=1}^{n} s_j \left( \sum_{i=1}^{m} a_{ij} t_{n+i} - c_j \right) + \sum_{i=1}^{m} \left( b_i - \sum_{j=1}^{n} a_{ij} s_j \right) t_{n+i}$$

$$= \sum_{j=1}^{n} \left( \sum_{i=1}^{m} a_{ij} s_j t_{n+i} \right) - \sum_{j=1}^{n} c_j s_j + \sum_{i=1}^{m} b_i t_{n+i}$$

$$\quad - \sum_{i=1}^{m} \left( \sum_{j=1}^{n} a_{ij} s_j t_{n+i} \right).$$

The last two "iterated sums" differ only in the order of summation and can easily be shown to be equal. We are therefore left with the two desired terms.   □

**Lemma 2.** *Suppose problems $\mathcal{P}$ and $\mathcal{P}^*$ are both feasible. Then any feasible value of $f$ is less than or equal to any feasible value of $g$.*

*Proof.* With the notation of Lemma 1, $s_k \geq 0$ and $t_k \geq 0$ for all $k$ from 1 to $n + m$. Therefore $\sum_{k=1}^{n+m} s_k t_k \geq 0$ and $f(s_1, \ldots, s_n) \leq g(t_{n+1}, \ldots, t_{n+m})$ as required.   □

The following corollary (mainly of the duality theorem) gives us the conclusion of the duality theorem under a different and possibly more convenient hypothesis.

**Corollary 1.** *Suppose dual problems $\mathcal{P}$ and $\mathcal{P}^*$ are both feasible. Then both problems have OFSs, and $\max f = \min g$.*

*Proof.* By Lemma 2, any feasible value of $g$ is an upper bound of $f$. Hence the only possible outcome for problem $\mathcal{P}$ is optimality. [The exact proof of this statement requires the transfer of relevant information between problems $\mathcal{P}$ and $\mathcal{E}(\mathcal{P})$, and the application of Theorem 4 of Chapter 4 to $\mathcal{E}(\mathcal{P})$.] The duality theorem now establishes the remaining assertions.   □

The next corollary will be invoked on two future occasions.

**Corollary 2.** *Let $(s_1, \ldots, s_n)$ and $(t_{n+1}, \ldots, t_{n+m})$ be feasible solutions of problems $\mathcal{P}$ and $\mathcal{P}^*$, respectively. Then $f(s_1, \ldots, s_n) = g(t_{n+1}, \ldots, t_{n+m})$ if and only if these feasible solutions are OFSs of their respective problems.*

*Proof.* Suppose the specified equation holds. Let $(r_1, \ldots, r_n)$ be an arbitrary feasible solution of $\mathcal{P}$. By Lemma 2 we conclude that

$$f(r_1, \ldots, r_n) \leq g(t_{n+1}, \ldots, t_{n+m}) = f(s_1, \ldots, s_n).$$

Hence $f(s_1, \ldots, s_n) = \max f$, and $(s_1, \ldots, s_n)$ is by definition an OFS of problem $\mathcal{P}$. By an analogous argument $g(t_{n+1}, \ldots, t_{n+m}) = \min g$. Thus both given feasible solutions are OFSs.

Conversely, if both are OFSs, then $f(s_1, \ldots, s_n) = \max f$, $g(t_{n+1}, \ldots, t_{n+m}) = \min g$, and the duality theorem gives the required equation.   □

In the last two corollaries and the last two lemmas we have assumed feasibility of both $\mathcal{P}$ and $\mathcal{P}^*$. Both problems then have OFSs. We now begin to determine precisely which outcomes are simultaneously possible for $\mathcal{P}$ and $\mathcal{P}^*$.

**Lemma 3.** *If either problem $\mathscr{P}$ or $\mathscr{P}*$ is "unbounded," the other is infeasible. (More precisely: If $f$ is unbounded above, $\mathscr{P}*$ is infeasible; if $g$ is unbounded below, $\mathscr{P}$ is infeasible.)*

*Proof.* Let $f$ be unbounded above. If $\mathscr{P}*$ had a feasible solution $(t_{n+1}, \ldots, t_{n+m})$, $g(t_{n+1}, \ldots, t_{n+m})$ would be an upper bound of $f$ (Lemma 2). Since this is impossible, $\mathscr{P}*$ is infeasible. The rest is similar. □

**Lemma 4.** *It is possible for both of two dual problems to be infeasible.*

*Proof.* An example (to which we shall return) follows:

$$\mathscr{P}: \begin{cases} \text{Maximize} & f(x_1, x_2) = x_1, \\ & x_2 \le -1, \qquad x_1, x_2 \ge 0. \\ & -x_1 + x_2 \le 0, \end{cases}$$

$$\mathscr{P}*: \begin{cases} \text{Minimize} & g(y_3, y_4) = -y_3, \\ & -y_4 \ge 1, \qquad y_3, y_4 \ge 0. \\ & y_3 + y_4 \ge 0, \end{cases} \qquad □$$

**Theorem 3.** *There are exactly four possible joint outcomes for dual problems $\mathscr{P}$ and $\mathscr{P}*$, namely, those indicated by the following chart:*

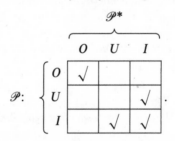

*(Both have OFSs, both are infeasible, either is unbounded while the other is infeasible.)*

*Proof.* First of all, outcomes $O$, $U$, and $I$ are the only possible individual outcomes for each of $\mathscr{P}$ and $\mathscr{P}*$. [One applies Theorem 4 of Chapter 4 to $\mathscr{E}(\mathscr{P})$ and $\mathscr{E}(\mathscr{P}*)$.] Next, $O$ for either problem implies $O$ for the other (duality theorem), and $U$ for either problem implies $I$ for the other (Lemma 3). Thus, all joint outcomes except the four specified have been eliminated.

It remains to make sure that examples of the four remaining possibilities actually exist. However, examples of $(O, O)$ are abundant, $(I, I)$ was demonstrated in Lemma 4, and examples of the other two joint outcomes are easily constructed. For instance, if the objective function of problem $\mathscr{P}$ in Lemma 4 is replaced by $f(x_1, x_2) = -x_1$, then $\mathscr{P}$ remains infeasible and $\mathscr{P}*$ becomes unbounded. □

It is sometimes stated (for instance, in this book) that solving one of two dual LP problems automatically solves the other. We have seen that this is true if the solved problem ends in optimality. Indeed, from the final tableau of the enlarged problem we can read off OFSs of both $\mathscr{P}$ and $\mathscr{P}^*$, as well as the common value of max $f$ and min $g$. We also know now that if either problem proves to be unbounded, the other must be infeasible. It is possible, however, to demonstrate infeasibility of either $\mathscr{P}$ or $\mathscr{P}^*$ and not know, without additional computation, whether the remaining problem is infeasible or unbounded. Problem 9 effectively illustrates this possibility.

The final theorem of the chapter is a striking, easily proved characterization of joint optimality. Several applications follow the theorem.

**Theorem 4** (Complementary Slackness Theorem). *Feasible solutions $(s_1, \ldots, s_n)$ and $(t_{n+1}, \ldots, t_{n+m})$ of $\mathscr{P}$ and $\mathscr{P}^*$, respectively, are both optimal if and only if the corresponding feasible solutions $(s_1, \ldots, s_{n+m})$ and $(t_1, \ldots, t_{n+m})$ of $\mathscr{E}(\mathscr{P})$ and $\mathscr{E}(\mathscr{P}^*)$, respectively, satisfy the complementary slackness (CS) conditions*

$$s_k t_k = 0, \qquad k = 1, \ldots, n + m. \tag{CS}$$

*(For each $k$, at least one of $s_k$ and $t_k$ is zero. One is the value of a decision variable; the other is the value of a slack variable.)*

*Proof.* Since $s_k$ and $t_k$ are nonnegative for every $k$ from 1 to $n + m$, (CS) is equivalent to $\sum_{k=1}^{n+m} s_k t_k = 0$. By Lemma 1, the latter equation is equivalent in turn to $f(s_1, \ldots, s_n) = g(t_{n+1}, \ldots, t_{n+m})$. Finally, Corollary 2 asserts that the last equation is equivalent to the simultaneous optimality of $(s_1, \ldots, s_n)$ and $(t_{n+1}, \ldots, t_{n+m})$.  $\square$

We now examine some examples, keeping in mind that the joint optimality of $(s_1, \ldots, s_n)$ and $(t_{n+1}, \ldots, t_{n+m})$ is equivalent to that of $(s_1, \ldots, s_{n+m})$ and $(t_1, \ldots, t_{n+m})$ in the respective enlarged problems. Let

|   | 5 | 6 | 7 | 8 |    |
|---|---|---|---|---|----|
| 1 | 3 | 7 |   |   | 11 |
| 2 | −5 | 4 |  |   | 0  |
| 3 | 2 | −3 |  |   | 0  |
| 4 | 3 | 8 |   |   | 12 |
| F | 0 | 0 | 9 | 10 |   |

be the final tableau of a problem $\mathscr{E}(\mathscr{P})$, blanks indicating irrelevant entries. The basic solution of this tableau is an OFS of $\mathscr{E}(\mathscr{P})$, and that of the dual tableau is an OFS of $\mathscr{E}(\mathscr{P}^*)$. These OFSs are $(11, 0, 0, 12, 0, 0, 0, 0)$ and $(0, 0, 0, 0, 0, 0, 9, 10)$, respectively. As assured by the CS theorem, one or both of these 8-tuples supplies a zero for each of the eight positions. However, it is obvious without any theorem that the conditions $s_k t_k = 0$ hold whenever $(s_1, \ldots, s_{n+m})$ and $(t_1, \ldots, t_{n+m})$ are the respective basic solutions of any pair of dual tableaux. Indeed, any subscript $k$ must lie along the top of one of the two tableaux. Therefore one of the variables $x_k$ or $y_k$ is nonbasic in its tableau. The value of this variable, either $s_k$ or $t_k$, is then zero in the basic solution.

For a more substantial illustration of the CS theorem we observe that $(1, 1, 1, 1, 1, 1, 0, 0)$ is a feasible solution of the problem $\mathscr{E}(\mathscr{P})$ above. Moreover, since the values here of $x_7$ and $x_8$ are zero, it is clear from the formula for $F$ that $(1, 1, 1, 1, 1, 1, 0, 0)$ is an OFS of $\mathscr{E}(\mathscr{P})$. Therefore, by the CS theorem, any OFS of $\mathscr{E}(\mathscr{P}^*)$ must have the form $(0, 0, 0, 0, 0, 0, t_7, t_8)$. In particular, the variables $y_1, \ldots, y_4$ must have the value zero. But $y_1, \ldots, y_4$ are all nonbasic in the dual tableau. Therefore the only feasible solution of $\mathscr{E}(\mathscr{P}^*)$ in which $y_1, \ldots, y_4$ all have the value zero is the basic solution of the dual tableau, namely, $(0, 0, 0, 0, 0, 0, 9, 10)$. Thus, unlike $\mathscr{E}(\mathscr{P})$, $\mathscr{E}(\mathscr{P}^*)$ has a unique OFS.

Let us next discuss an example without tableaux, and one strongly illustrating the sufficiency, as well as the necessity, of the CS conditions. Suppose it is asserted that the problem

$$\mathscr{P}: \quad \begin{cases} \text{Maximize} \quad f(x_1, x_2) = -8x_1 + 9x_2, \\[1mm] \qquad x_1 - 6x_2 \le \quad 3, \\[1mm] \quad -2x_1 + \quad x_2 \le -1, \\[1mm] \quad -4x_1 + 5x_2 \le \quad 2, \end{cases} \qquad x_1, x_2 \ge 0.$$

was solved graphically, and that $(\frac{7}{6}, \frac{4}{3})$ was found to be an OFS. We can use the CS theorem to determine whether $(\frac{7}{6}, \frac{4}{3})$ is an OFS of $\mathscr{P}$ as follows. First we check that $(\frac{7}{6}, \frac{4}{3})$ is feasible:

$$\tfrac{7}{6} - 6(\tfrac{4}{3}) = -\tfrac{41}{6} < 3,$$

$$-2(\tfrac{7}{6}) + \tfrac{4}{3} = -1,$$

$$-4(\tfrac{7}{6}) + 5(\tfrac{4}{3}) = 2.$$

While establishing feasibility, these calculations also give the slack variable values $\frac{59}{6}$, 0, 0. Thus, $(\frac{7}{6}, \frac{4}{3}, \frac{59}{6}, 0, 0)$ is the feasible solution of $\mathscr{E}(\mathscr{P})$ corresponding to $(\frac{7}{6}, \frac{4}{3})$.

Now, if we can find a feasible solution $(t_1, t_2, t_3, t_4, t_5)$ of $\mathscr{E}(\mathscr{P}^*)$, with $t_1 = t_2 = t_3 = 0$, the CS condition will hold. This will prove that $(\frac{7}{6}, \frac{4}{3})$ is indeed an OFS. Conversely, if $(\frac{7}{6}, \frac{4}{3})$ is an OFS of $\mathscr{P}$, the duality theorem ensures the existence of an OFS $(t_3, t_4, t_5)$ of $\mathscr{P}^*$. There then corresponds an OFS $(t_1, t_2, t_3, t_4, t_5)$ of $\mathscr{E}(\mathscr{P}^*)$, and the CS conditions again yield $t_1 = t_2 = t_3 = 0$. The import of this converse statement is that our search for $(t_1, \ldots, t_5)$ will not be in vain if $(\frac{7}{6}, \frac{4}{3})$ really is an OFS of $\mathscr{P}$. To summarize, $(\frac{7}{6}, \frac{4}{3})$ is an OFS of $\mathscr{P}$ if and only if there exists a feasible solution of $\mathscr{E}(\mathscr{P}^*)$ of the form $(0, 0, 0, t_4, t_5)$.

We must now look at the constraints of $\mathscr{E}(\mathscr{P}^*)$. Since $\mathscr{P}^*$ contains the constraints

$$y_3 - 2y_4 - 4y_5 \geq -8,$$
$$-6y_3 + y_4 + 5y_5 \geq 9,$$

the equality constraints of $\mathscr{E}(\mathscr{P}^*)$ are

$$y_1 - y_3 + 2y_4 + 4y_5 = 8,$$
$$y_2 + 6y_3 - y_4 - 5y_5 = -9.$$

Therefore, a 5-tuple of the form $(0, 0, 0, t_4, t_5)$ is a feasible solution of $\mathscr{E}(\mathscr{P}^*)$ if and only if $t_4 \geq 0, t_5 \geq 0$, and the equations

$$2t_4 + 4t_5 = 8,$$
$$-t_4 - 5t_5 = -9,$$

both hold. It follows that $(0, 0, 0, \frac{2}{3}, \frac{5}{3})$ (and no other 5-tuple) is a feasible solution of $\mathscr{E}(\mathscr{P}^*)$ of the required form. We have therefore proved that $(\frac{7}{6}, \frac{4}{3})$ is an OFS of $\mathscr{P}$ [and incidentally that $(0, \frac{2}{3}, \frac{5}{3})$ is the unique OFS of $\mathscr{P}^*$].

We conclude the chapter by attempting to answer the following question about the production problem: *How is the maximum profit affected by small changes in the available amounts of the resources?* To again making the question precise and to ensure our ultimate success in answering it, we assume we are given an initial production problem $\mathscr{P}$ with the property that $\mathscr{P}^*$ *has a unique OFS.* One can attempt to verify this property in a given example by solving $\mathscr{E}(\mathscr{P})$ by SIMPLEX. If an optimal tableau with all positive constants is reached, the desired uniqueness is ensured (Problem 21 of Chapter 3), and the OFS in question can be read off the dual tableau. If one or more of the constants are zero, the uniqueness question requires further investigation.

The next step is to formulate a modification of $\mathscr{P}$ that appropriately reflects the "small changes" in the supply of the resources. Let $\mathscr{P}$ be given with the usual notation: $f, a_{ij}, b_i, c_j$ $(i = 1, \ldots, m; j = 1, \ldots, n)$. The definition of the constants $a_{ij}$ is independent of the available amounts of the resources. These same constants, therefore, should appear and play the same role in the modified problem. We also assume that the unit net profits $c_j$ associated with the various products are unaffected by small changes in the available amounts of the resources. This assumption seems consistent with the following scenario (to which we shall return): The manufacturer purchases the resources at certain prices, and the unit prices are unchanged if slightly different amounts of the resources are purchased.

In accordance with this discussion, we postulate an LP problem *differing from the given problem $\mathscr{P}$ only in the right-hand constants of the constraints.* To express this difference, we let $\varepsilon_1, \ldots, \varepsilon_m$ be real numbers of "small" absolute value. (More about *how* small latter, but a precise discussion of an upper bound for $|\varepsilon_1|, \ldots, |\varepsilon_m|$ is beyond our reach.) Finally, we let $\varepsilon$ denote the

$m$-tuple $(\varepsilon_1, \ldots, \varepsilon_m)$, and $\mathscr{P}_\varepsilon$ the following problem:

$$\mathscr{P}_\varepsilon: \begin{cases} \text{Maximize} \quad f_\varepsilon(x_1, \ldots, x_n) = \sum_{j=1}^{n} c_j x_j \\ \text{subject to} \quad \sum_{j=1}^{n} a_{ij} x_j \leq b_i + \varepsilon_i, \qquad i = 1, \ldots, m, \\ \qquad\qquad\qquad x_j \geq 0, \qquad\qquad\qquad j = 1, \ldots, n. \end{cases}$$

We have denoted the objective functions of $\mathscr{P}$ and $\mathscr{P}_\varepsilon$ by different symbols because their domains are (in general) different. It is this difference in domain that makes it difficult to analyze $\mathscr{P}_\varepsilon$ when $\varepsilon$ deviates from $(0, \ldots, 0)$. However, by the device of studying the dual problem $\mathscr{P}_\varepsilon^*$ instead of $\mathscr{P}_\varepsilon$ itself, we shall easily achieve our goal! Indeed, we shall succeed in expressing $\max f_\varepsilon$ as a simple (linear plus constant) function of $\varepsilon$.

The LP problem $\mathscr{P}_\varepsilon^*$ is the following:

$$\mathscr{P}_\varepsilon: \begin{cases} \text{Minimize} \quad g_\varepsilon(y_{n+1}, \ldots, y_{n+m}) = \sum_{i=1}^{m} (b_i + \varepsilon_i) y_{n+i} \\ \text{subject to} \quad \sum_{i=1}^{m} a_{ij} y_{n+i} \geq c_j, \qquad j = 1, \ldots, n, \\ \qquad\qquad\qquad y_{n+i} \geq 0, \qquad\qquad i = 1, \ldots, m. \end{cases}$$

Roughly put, we shall find it easier to analyze an objective function $(g_\varepsilon)$ with a varying formula and a fixed domain than one $(f_\varepsilon)$ with a fixed formula and a varying domain. The duality theorem will then enable us to transfer our conclusions concerning $g_\varepsilon$ to $f_\varepsilon$.

More precisely, let $(t_{n+1}, \ldots, t_{n+m})$ be the postulated unique OFS of $\mathscr{P}^*$. It can then be proved that $(t_{n+1}, \ldots, t_{n+m})$ is also an OFS of $\mathscr{P}_\varepsilon^*$ if $|\varepsilon_1|, \ldots, |\varepsilon_m|$ are all sufficiently small. For all such $\varepsilon$, this means that

$$\min g_\varepsilon = g_\varepsilon(t_{n+1}, \ldots, t_{n+m}) = \sum_{i=1}^{m} b_i t_{n+i} + \sum_{i=1}^{m} \varepsilon_i t_{n+i}.$$

By the duality theorem, $\max f_\varepsilon = \min g_\varepsilon$, and in particular, $\max f = \sum_{i=1}^{m} b_i t_{n+i}$. Hence

$$\max f_\varepsilon = \max f + \sum_{i=1}^{m} t_{n+i} \varepsilon_i.$$

Our answer to the original question, under all the assumptions we have made, is therefore as follows: *If the available amount of each resource $R_i$ is changed by $\varepsilon_i$ units, then the maximum profit changes by $\sum_{i=1}^{m} t_{n+i} \varepsilon_i$ dollars.*

We can also say that for small changes in availability of the resources, total net profits increase at the rate of $t_{n+i}$ dollars per *unit* increase of $R_i$. Consequently, as long as $(t_{n+i}, \ldots, t_{n+m})$ remains an OFS of $\mathscr{P}_\varepsilon^*$, *the manufacturer could pay up to $t_{n+i}$ dollars more than usual per additional unit of $R_i$, and still come out ahead.* The number $t_{n+i}$ is therefore called the *marginal value* or *shadow price* of resource $R_i$. A numerical example concerning marginal values appears in Problem 15.

It remains to comment upon the case of a zero marginal value. Suppose for some OFS $(s_1, \ldots, s_n)$ of $\mathscr{P}$, one of the constraints of $\mathscr{P}$ holds as an inequality. For ease of notation, let it be the first constraint: $\sum_{j=1}^{n} a_{1j}s_j < b_1$. In industrial language, $R_1$ is an underutilized resource in the optimal production schedule defined by $(s_1, \ldots, s_n)$. Intuition then suggests that a small increase in the availability of $R_1$ will not lead to an increase in the maximum profit. This feeling is confirmed by an application of the CS theorem. Namely, with our usual notation we are supposing that $s_{n+1} \neq 0$. It must be the case, therefore, that $t_{n+1} = 0$; that is, the marginal value of the resource $R_1$ is zero. Hence $t_{n+1}\varepsilon_1$, the increase in profit resulting from a small increase $\varepsilon_1$ in the amount of $R_1$, is also zero.

Actually, even an arbitrarily large increase in the amount of resource $R_1$ cannot increase maximum profit. To prove this statement, we continue, of course, to assume the existence of the OFS $(s_1, \ldots, s_n)$ described above. On the other hand, we no longer need the assumption that $\mathscr{P}^*$ has a unique OFS. The duality theorem ensures the existence of at least one OFS of $\mathscr{P}^*$, and we shall use this fact in our proof.

With the notation we have established, the statement to be proved is the following: If $\varepsilon_1$ is any positive number (no matter how large) and $\varepsilon$ is the $m$-tuple $(\varepsilon_1, 0, \ldots, 0)$, then $\max f_\varepsilon$ exists and equals $\max f$. For the proof we let $(u_{n+1}, \ldots, u_{n+m})$ be an arbitrary feasible solution of $\mathscr{P}^*$ (or, equivalently, of $\mathscr{P}_\varepsilon^*$). Then

$$g(u_{n+1}, \ldots, u_{b+m}) = \sum_{i=1}^{m} b_i u_{n+i} \leq (b_1 + \varepsilon_1)u_{n+1} + \sum_{i=2}^{m} b_i u_{n+i}$$

$$= g_\varepsilon(u_{n+1}, \ldots, u_{n+m}).$$

Next, let $(t_{n+1}, \ldots, t_{n+m})$ be an OFS of $\mathscr{P}^*$. Again, the assumption that $s_{n+1} \neq 0$ implies that $t_{n+1} = 0$. Therefore

$$g(t_{n+1}, \ldots, t_{n+m}) = \sum_{i=2}^{m} b_i t_{n+i} = g_\varepsilon(t_{n+1}, \ldots, t_{n+m}).$$

Since $g(t_{n+1}, \ldots, t_{n+m}) \leq g(u_{n+1}, \ldots, u_{n+m})$, we conclude that $g_\varepsilon(t_{n+1}, \ldots, t_{n+m}) \leq g_\varepsilon(u_{n+1}, \ldots, u_{n+m})$. Thus $(t_{n+1}, \ldots, t_{n+m})$ is an OFS of $\mathscr{P}_\varepsilon^*$, and $\min g_\varepsilon = \min g$. Finally, by the duality theorem, $\max f_\varepsilon = \max f$, as asserted. This completes our discussion.

## PROBLEMS

1. Write down the dual $\mathscr{P}^*$ of the LP problem $\mathscr{P}$ below. (For later reference denote the objective function of $\mathscr{P}^*$ by $g$.)

$$\mathscr{P}: \begin{cases} \text{Maximize} & f(x_1, x_2, x_3) = 4x_1 - 3x_2 \\ \text{subject to} & 2x_2 - 3x_3 \leq -1, \qquad x_1, x_2, x_3 \geq 0. \\ & 5x_1 \quad + \ x_3 \leq \ 2, \end{cases}$$

2. For the problems $\mathscr{P}$ and $\mathscr{P}^*$ of Problem 1, write down $\mathscr{E}(\mathscr{P})$ and $\mathscr{E}(\mathscr{P}^*)$. Then check your accuracy by determining whether the condensed tableau representations are dual tableaux.

3. Give a general demonstration, as outlined in the text, that "the dual of the dual is the primal."

4. For a certain problem $\mathscr{P}$ in primal form, NNA–SIMPLEX was applied to $\mathscr{E}(\mathscr{P})$, and the tableau

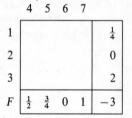

was reached. Solve both $\mathscr{P}$ and $\mathscr{P}^*$.

   *Answer*: $\max f = f(\frac{1}{4}, 0, 2, 0) = -3 = g(\frac{3}{4}, 0, 1) = \min g$.

5. The diet problem specified by the chart

|        | $F_1$ | $F_2$ | MDR |
|--------|-------|-------|-----|
| $N_1$  | 5     | 1     | 11  |
| $N_2$  | 2     | 1     | 8   |
| $N_3$  | 1     | 2     | 7   |
| cents/pound | 40 | 30 | |

has been considered in previous problem sections (Chapters 2 and 4). Solve it now as follows:

   (i) Write out the problem with variables $y_4$ and $y_5$.
   (ii) Recognize the result as the dual $\mathscr{P}^*$ of a primal problem $\mathscr{P}$.
   (iii) Solve $\mathscr{E}(\mathscr{P})$ by SIMPLEX. (Suggestion: Keep $x_1$ nonbasic.)
   (iv) From your final tableau, determine the necessary information about $\mathscr{P}^*$.

6. Let $\mathscr{P}$ and $\mathscr{P}^*$ be the dual problems of Problem 1.

   (a) Find by inspection one feasible solution of each problem.
   (b) Compute the corresponding feasible values of $f$ and $g$, respectively.
   (c) Compare your results and thereby illustrate Lemma 2.
   (d) Determine the feasible solutions of $\mathscr{E}(\mathscr{P})$ and $\mathscr{E}(\mathscr{P}^*)$ corresponding to your feasible solutions of $\mathscr{P}$ and $\mathscr{P}^*$, respectively.
   (e) Verify the identity of Lemma 1 using your results from parts (b) and (d).

7. For $\mathscr{P}$ and $\mathscr{P}^*$ of Problems 1 and 6, verify that $(\frac{1}{3}, 0, \frac{1}{3})$ and $(\frac{4}{15}, \frac{4}{5})$, respectively, are feasible solutions. Show further that $f(\frac{1}{3}, 0, \frac{1}{3}) = g(\frac{4}{15}, \frac{4}{5})$. What is your conclusion?

8. To obtain $(\frac{1}{3}, 0, \frac{1}{3})$ and $(\frac{4}{15}, \frac{4}{5})$ for yourself, or for more practice solving dual LP problems simultaneously, solve both $\mathscr{P}$ and $\mathscr{P}^*$ of Problems 1, 2, 6, and 7 by applying NNA–SIMPLEX to either $\mathscr{E}(\mathscr{P})$ or $\mathscr{E}(\mathscr{P}^*)$.

9. For a certain problem $\mathscr{P}$ in primal form, NNA was applied to $\mathscr{E}(\mathscr{P})$, and the tableau

|  | 6 | 1 | 5 |  |
|---|---|---|---|---|
| 4 | 1 | 0 | 0 | −1 |
| 2 | −1 | 2 | −1 | 3 |
| 3 | 2 | −3 | 1 | 4 |
| F | 8 | 6 | −2 | 9 |

was obtained. The first row shows that $\mathscr{E}(\mathscr{P})$ and therefore $\mathscr{P}$ are infeasible. The dual tableau represents $\mathscr{E}(\mathscr{P}^*)$, but it is not a "final tableau." Thus, even though $\mathscr{P}$ is solved, the outcome of $\mathscr{P}^*$ is still in doubt. All these statements continue to hold if the objective entry 6 is replaced by 5.99. Show that in the first situation $\mathscr{P}^*$ is unbounded, but that in the second, $\mathscr{P}^*$ is infeasible.

10. Verify that $(4, 1)$ is an OFS of the problem

$$\mathscr{P}: \begin{cases} \text{Maximize} \quad f(x_1, x_2) = 3x_1 - 2x_2, \\ -x_1 + x_2 \le 2, \\ x_1 - x_2 \le 3, \qquad\qquad x_1, x_2 \ge 0, \\ 2x_1 + 3x_2 \le 11, \end{cases}$$

and simultaneously find an OFS of $\mathscr{P}^*$ by using the CS conditions. (Follow the method of the text.)
   *Answer:* $(0, \frac{13}{5}, \frac{1}{5})$.

11. Try the same procedure with the feasible solution $(1, 3)$ in place of $(4, 1)$. What goes wrong?

12. Prove that no matter what constants $b_1$, $b_2$, $b_3$ appear in place of 2, 3, 11, respectively, in Problem 10, there cannot be an OFS $(s_1, s_2)$ of problem $\mathscr{P}$ with either of the following two properties:

   (i) $s_2 > 0$ and $s_1 - s_2 < b_2$.
   (ii) $2s_1 + 3s_2 < b_3$.

13. In Problem 10, let the constant 11 be replaced by 6. The resulting problem $\mathscr{P}$ then has the (unique) OFS $(3, 0)$. Use this information and the CS conditions to find infinitely many OFSs of $\mathscr{P}^*$.
   *Answer:* $(0, 5t - 1, 0, -2t + 3, t)$ with $\frac{1}{5} \le t \le \frac{3}{2}$.

14. Consider the problem

$$\mathscr{P}: \begin{cases} \text{Maximize} \quad f(x_1, x_2, x_3) = 4x_1 - 5x_2 + 7x_3, \\ 3x_1 - x_2 + x_3 \le -2, \\ -5x_1 + x_3 \le 8, \qquad\qquad x_1, x_2, x_3 \ge 0. \\ 6x_1 - 4x_2 + 5x_3 \le -7, \end{cases}$$

There are reasons to believe that there is an OFS for which all the $\leq$ constraints hold with equality. Assuming that this is correct, use the CS conditions to find an OFS of $\mathscr{P}^*$.

*Answer*: (1, 1, 1).

15. Let $\mathscr{P}$ denote the boat production problem in Chapter 2, Problem 1, and Chapter 3, Problem 18. Apply the discussion of marginal values to $\mathscr{P}$. Begin by checking that $\mathscr{P}^*$ has a unique OFS, namely, (4, 10, 60). Show that the maximum monthly net profit equals

$$(630 + \varepsilon_1)4 + (110 + \varepsilon_2)10 + (50 + \varepsilon_3)60 = g_\varepsilon(4, 10, 60),$$

under the indicated small changes in the supply of the resources, as long as (4, 10, 60) remains an OFS when $g_\varepsilon$ replaces $g$. In particular, the maximum profit increases by 4 dollars for each additional pound of aluminum the manufacturer can obtain (bought at the usual price per pound). Also, each additional hour obtainable in section 2 of the workshop increases net profits by 60 dollars.

# CHAPTER 6

# Matrix Games

Let us begin with an example (diagram below). Suppose two people, Rose and Colin, play the following game: Rose has two cards labeled 1 and 4, respectively; Colin has cards labeled 1, 2, and 3. Each player knows the holdings of the other. Rose secretly selects one of her two cards, Colin one of his three. Then the two players simultaneously display their choices. If the sum of the two selected cards is even, Rose wins that many dollars from Colin; if the sum is odd, Colin wins that amount from Rose. The following diagram summarizes these rules *from Rose's point of view*.

$$
\begin{array}{c}
\text{Colin's choices} \\[4pt]
\overbrace{\begin{array}{ccc} 1 & 2 & 3 \end{array}}
\end{array}
$$

$$
\text{Rose's choices} \quad \begin{array}{c} 1 \\ 4 \end{array} \left[ \begin{array}{ccc} 2 & -3 & 4 \\ -5 & 6 & -7 \end{array} \right].
$$

For instance, if Rose chooses 4 and Colin chooses 3, we are led to the entry $-7$, which represents a loss of 7 dollars for Rose. This agrees with our rule about an odd sum.

The six matrix entries above are referred to as Rose's *payoffs*, a negative payoff always representing a loss for Rose and a gain for Colin. We could, in addition, construct the corresponding diagram showing Colin's payoffs, but this would be unnecessary because whatever one player wins, the other loses. Thus we can make do with the payoff diagram of just one of the players, whom we permanently fix to be Rose.

The following reasoning shows that our game and diagram can be somewhat streamlined. If Rose chooses card 4, for example, her payoff will be $-5$, 6, or $-7$, depending on what Colin does. In effect, Rose is choosing the bottom row of the matrix as the source of her payoff. Likewise, Colin's choice of a card determines the *column* of Rose's payoff. Therefore we can dispense with the cards, the column headings, and the row headings. We then concentrate on the matrix

$$A = \begin{bmatrix} 2 & -3 & 4 \\ -5 & 6 & -7 \end{bmatrix},$$

with the understanding that *Rose simply selects one of the rows of A, and Colin selects a column.* The appropriate payoff can then be easily determined. This matrix provides all the essential information of the game; we can forget about the physical objects with which the game is played and about the rules for determining the payoffs. The game thus streamlined is called a *matrix game*, and the matrix $A$ is called the *payoff matrix* of the game or *Rose's payoff matrix*. The reader has probably noticed that the names Rose and Colin help us remember who chooses rows and who chooses columns.

The problem, roughly stated, for each of the two players of a matrix game is the following: What choice (choices, if the game is played more than once) should I make in order for my partial influence over the outcome to benefit me the most? We defer the discussion of this question pending the presentation of a few more examples. Much remains to be clarified before this question can be answered.

A simple and perhaps familiar game is that of "Matching Pennies." Each of the two players has a penny, and each simultaneously shows either "heads" (H) or "tails" (T). If there is a match (both H or both T), Rose wins 1 dollar from Colin. Otherwise, Colin wins 1 dollar from Rose. Rose's diagram and payoff matrix $A$ are then the following:

$$\text{Colin}$$

$$\begin{array}{cc} & \text{H} \quad \text{T} \end{array}$$

$$\text{Rose} \begin{array}{c} \text{H} \\ \text{T} \end{array} \begin{bmatrix} 1 & -1 \\ -1 & 1 \end{bmatrix}, \qquad A = \begin{bmatrix} 1 & -1 \\ -1 & 1 \end{bmatrix}.$$

Our next example is the game Paper–Rock–Scissors. Each of the two players has these three choices, and the winner of the showdown is suggested by the following rules: Paper covers rock; rock breaks scissors; scissors cuts paper. The payoffs (to Rose) are determined by the diagram below, there being no payment if both players make the same choice.

$$\text{Colin}$$

$$\begin{array}{ccc} & \text{P} \quad \text{R} \quad \text{S} \end{array}$$

$$\text{Rose} \begin{array}{c} \text{P} \\ \text{R} \\ \text{S} \end{array} \begin{bmatrix} 0 & 1 & -2 \\ -1 & 0 & 1 \\ 2 & -1 & 0 \end{bmatrix}.$$

A seemingly different game has Rose and Colin each extend one, two, or three fingers. If the difference in the number of fingers is 0, the payoff is 0; if the difference is 1, the player putting forth the *smaller* number of fingers wins one dollar; and if the difference is 2, the player showing the *larger* number wins two dollars. The diagram follows:

Colin

$$
\text{Rose} \left\{
\begin{array}{c}
\phantom{}\\
\phantom{}\\
\phantom{}
\end{array}
\right.
\begin{array}{c}
1\\
2\\
3
\end{array}
\begin{array}{ccc}
1 & 2 & 3\\
\end{array}
\left[
\begin{array}{ccc}
0 & 1 & -2\\
-1 & 0 & 1\\
2 & -1 & 0
\end{array}
\right].
$$

Thus we arrive at the payoff matrix

$$
A = \left[
\begin{array}{ccc}
0 & 1 & -2\\
-1 & 0 & 1\\
2 & -1 & 0
\end{array}
\right]
$$

for both of these games. This discussion shows that our policy of reducing various games to the game of selecting rows and columns of a payoff matrix can reveal that two apparently different games are mathematically identical. We can hope, therefore, to analyze both games simultaneously.

Having read through these examples of matrix games, the student will have a sense of the scope of the following definition. (The definition is not a strictly mathematical one; we later summarize the mathematical content of our definitions.)

**Definition 1.** Given any matrix

$$
A = \left[
\begin{array}{ccc}
a_{11} & \cdots & a_{1n}\\
\vdots & & \vdots\\
a_{m1} & \cdots & a_{mn}
\end{array}
\right],
\tag{1}
$$

the $m \times n$ *matrix game* $\Gamma_A$ *with payoff matrix A* is played by two persons, Rose and Colin, as follows: Rose selects a row of $A$, Colin a column. If Rose chooses row $i$ $(1 \le i \le m)$ and Colin chooses column $j$ $(1 \le j \le n)$, then *Rose's payoff* is $a_{ij}$. More explicitly: If $a_{ij} > 0$, Colin pays Rose $a_{ij}$ dollars; if $a_{ij} < 0$, Rose pays Colin $|a_{ij}|$ dollars; if $a_{ij} = 0$, no money is won or lost. The matrix $A$ is known to both players.

It should be clear that any game with the following three properties can be represented as a matrix game.

(i) There are two players.

(ii) Each player has finitely many choices of play, each makes one choice, and the combination of the two choices determines a payoff.

(iii) What one player wins, the other loses.

Of course, the converse is also true: The general matrix game $\Gamma_A$ of Definition 1 has properties (i) through (iii). Consequently, matrix games can be characterized as *finite, two-person, zero-sum, one-move games*.

We now begin to discuss how the players make their choices. None of the specific games described so far would have much mathematical interest if one of the palyers knew the opposing player's choice in advance. Even some sort of partial information could confer a significant advantage. Let us therefore imagine some of the ways, both offensive and defensive, in which the players could deal with this "security issue."

If a matrix game is played several times, one might look for a pattern in the opponent's choices. For instance, if Rose methodically alternates between heads and tails in the game Matching Pennies, Colin can take advantage in an obvious way (as long as Rose persists). Similarly, he may be able to capitalize upon any other nonrandom pattern in Rose's play. In the example $\Gamma_A$ with

$$A = \begin{bmatrix} 2 & -3 & 4 \\ -5 & 6 & -7 \end{bmatrix}$$

let us suppose that Rose consistently chooses row one. Colin could then begin playing only column two, thereby winning 3 dollars per game. We can imagine further: If Rose sees Colin favoring column two, she can start selecting row two in order to win 6 dollars. We can go on and on, imagining a never ending "instability."

This "aggressive" approach of seeking to exploit information about the opposing player's choices could conceivably be fruitful, but certain questions arise: How does the "aggressive" player make his/her own choices while studying the opponent's play? Will any discovered pattern continue after it is detected? What will happen if both players simultaneously try to find and exploit patterns in each other's play? Will a stable situation ever be reached? What if the game is to be played only one time? Is a mathematical analysis of matrix games in fact possible?

Let us now consider a "defensive" approach. The players could protect the security of their choices by making these choices randomly. For instance, if Colin has three columns from which to choose, he could decide to select them at random with probabilities (for example) $\frac{1}{2}$, $\frac{1}{3}$, and $\frac{1}{6}$, respectively. This could be accomplished by rolling a die and choosing column one if 1, 2, or 3 comes up; column two if 4 or 5 comes up; and column three if 6 comes up. By such a technique Colin would presumably be protected from producing nonrandom choice patterns in a series of plays of the game. Even if a matrix game is to be played only once, the randomness of a player's choice could offer protection against clever guessing or "mind reading."

The idea of selecting rows and columns according to fixed probabilities could apply even to certain perhaps atypical games (called *strictly determined*) in which secrecy of the players' choices is unimportant. For example, if

$$A = \begin{bmatrix} 3 & 2 \\ 0 & 1 \\ 1 & -1 \end{bmatrix},$$

it is intuitively clear that Rose should choose row one every time the game is played. Her "best" probabilities are then 1, 0, 0 for rows one, two, and three, respectively. (More on strictly determined games later.)

Motivated by the preceding considerations (and by the fact that a satisfying mathematical theory becomes possible), we henceforth assume that *whenever a matrix game is played, there exist probabilities with which the rows and columns are selected*. To make this precise we introduce Definitions 2 and 3.

**Definition 2.** For any positive integer $k$, let $\mathscr{S}_k$ be the set of all $k$-tuples of nonnegative numbers with sum 1. In symbols,

$$\mathscr{S}_k = \{(q_1, \ldots, q_k): q_1, \ldots, q_k \geq 0; q_1 + \cdots + q_k = 1\}.$$

For example, $(\frac{1}{2}, \frac{1}{3}, \frac{1}{6}) \in \mathscr{S}_3$. In general, given an $m \times n$ matrix game $\Gamma_A$, the relevance of $\mathscr{S}_m$ and $\mathscr{S}_n$ is clear: Each element of $\mathscr{S}_m$ provides a sequence of probabilities with which Rose can play the rows of $A$. The same applies for $\mathscr{S}_n$ and Colin.

**Definition 3.** Given an $m \times n$ matrix game $\Gamma_A$, a *strategy for Rose* is an element $r = (r_1, \ldots, r_m)$ of $\mathscr{S}_m$. Similarly, a *strategy for Colin* is an element $c = (c_1, \ldots, c_n)$ of $\mathscr{S}_n$. The statement that *Rose adopts strategy $r$ ($r \in \mathscr{S}_m$)* means that Rose selects one of the rows of $A$ at random in such a way that for every $i$ $(1 \leq i \leq m)$, the probability is $r_i$ that the $i$th row is selected. The statement that *Colin adopts strategy $c$ ($c \in \mathscr{S}_n$)* is analogously defined. If Rose adopts strategy $r$ and Colin adopts strategy $c$, then for every $i$ and $j$ $(1 \leq i \leq m, 1 \leq j \leq n)$, the probability of the joint event that row $i$ and column $j$ are selected is $r_i c_j$.

For the reader who understands the rudiments of probability theory, we remark that the combined mathematical content of Definitions 1 and 3 is essentially the following: For each $m \times n$ matrix $A$, each $r \in \mathscr{S}_m$, and each $c \in \mathscr{S}_n$, Rose's payoff is a random variable taking the values $a_{ij}$ $(1 \leq i \leq m, 1 \leq j \leq n)$ with probabilities $r_i c_j$. To produce this severe reduction of Definitions 1 and 3, we have removed the game-theoretic references and expressed the mathematical remainder as succinctly as possible.

Earlier, we very roughly stated the problem facing the players of a matrix game. Having agreed upon how the players make their choices, we can formulate the question slightly more precisely: What strategy (Definition 3) should each player adopt to achieve maximum benefit? Of course, we must now begin to define "maximum benefit". A necessary first step for this is to agree that both players are concerned only with the *expected values* of their payoffs. As was the case with payoff matrices, it will only be necessary to make a definition involving Rose. (This is again a consequence of the zero-sum aspect of matrix games.)

**Definition 4.** Let $\Gamma_A$ be an $m \times n$ matrix game as in (1). Then for each $r \in \mathscr{S}_m$ and $c \in \mathscr{S}_n$, *Rose's expected payoff*, denoted $E(r, c)$ or $E_A(r, c)$, is defined by

$$E(r, c) = \sum_{i=1}^{m} \sum_{j=1}^{n} a_{ij} r_i c_j. \tag{2}$$

To illustrate, if

$$A = \begin{array}{c} \\ r_1 \\ r_2 \\ r_3 \end{array} \begin{array}{ccc} c_1 & c_2 & c_3 \\ \left[ \begin{array}{ccc} 1 & -10 & 9 \\ 2 & 3 & 2 \\ 0 & 30 & -20 \end{array} \right], \end{array}$$

then

$$E(r, c) = r_1 c_1 - 10 r_1 c_2 + 9 r_1 c_3 + 2 r_2 c_1 + 3 r_2 c_2 + 2 r_2 c_3$$
$$+ 30 r_3 c_2 - 20 r_3 c_3.$$

As a computational aid we have attached the probabilities $r_1, r_2, r_3, c_1, c_2, c_3$ to the appropriate rows and columns. With these in place, $E(r, c)$ is the sum of all possible products containing as factors one row heading, one column heading, and the corresponding payoff entry.

Definition 4 is superfluous for the reader who knows the general definition of expected value and understands the description of Rose's payoff as a random variable. It is also clear that "Colin's expected payoff" is the negative of Rose's. The less well-versed reader is requested to accept the definition of $E(r, c)$ as a good measure of the worth to Rose of one play of the game, assuming the strategies $r$ and $c$ are adopted. Perhaps it will be helpful to add that Rose's payoffs would tend to average $E(r, c)$ per game if the game were played many times. (Precise versions of this statement can be found in the so-called laws of large numbers in the theory of probability.)

Using Definition 4 we can describe the players' goals as follows: Rose would like to adopt a strategy $r$ so that $E(r, c)$ is "as large as possible"; Colin wishes to choose $c$ so that $E(r, c)$ is "as small as possible." These statements still have no precise meaning, however. For instance, Rose cannot maximize a function of two (vector) variables when she can choose the value of only one of these variables. We shall proceed without formulating a precise statement of each player's goal, although we shall return to this point at the end of the chapter. Instead, let us now simply describe what each player can achieve in the struggle over $E(r, c)$.

Consider the example of Definition 4. If Rose adopts $(r_1', r_2', r_3') = (0, 1, 0)$, then $E(r', c) = 2c_1 + 3c_2 + 2c_3 \geq 2$ for all $c \in \mathscr{S}_3$. On the other hand, if Colin chooses $(c_1', c_2', c_3') = (\frac{7}{8}, 0, \frac{1}{8})$, then $E(r, c') = \frac{7}{8}r_1 + \frac{9}{8}r_1 + \frac{14}{8}r_2 + \frac{2}{8}r_2 - \frac{20}{8}r_3 = 2r_1 + 2r_2 - \frac{5}{2}r_3 \leq 2$ for all $r \in \mathcal{S}_3$. Thus, the number 2 appears both as a lower bound and an upper bound of Rose's expected payoff. Precisely and generally, we have the following theorem, the *Fundamental Theorem of Matrix Games* (*FTMG*).

**Theorem** (FTMG). *Let $\Gamma_A$ be an $m \times n$ matrix game. Then there is a unique number $v_A$ with the following property: Strategies $r' \in \mathcal{S}_m$ and $c' \in \mathcal{S}_n$ exist (uniqueness not asserted) such that*

$$E(r', c) \geq v_A \qquad \text{for all} \quad c \in \mathcal{S}_n, \tag{3}$$

*and*

$$E(r, c') \leq v_A \qquad \text{for all} \quad r \in \mathcal{S}_m. \tag{4}$$

*In particular,*

$$E(r', c') = v_A. \tag{5}$$

Inequality (3) states that Rose, by adopting the strategy $r'$, can be sure that her expected payoff is at least $v_A$ no matter what strategy Colin adopts. At the same time, according to (4), if Colin adopts strategy $c'$, he can be certain that Rose's expected payoff is no more than $v_A$. [Equivalently, he can make certain that his own expected payoff will be at least $-v_A$. To see the equivalence, we multiply (4) by $-1$ and apply our previous remark that Colin's expected payoff is the negative of Rose's.] The number $v_A$ is called the *value* of the game $\Gamma_A$.

Strategies $r'$ and $c'$, as in (3) and (4), are called *optimal strategies* (Definition 7 below). We shall see by example that a matrix game player, by adopting certain nonoptimal strategies, can try for a greater expected payoff then what is ensured. Such attempts, however, carry the risk of obtaining a smaller expected payoff. Thus there can be a choice between "conservative" and "speculative" play. The statement that Rose, for instance, plays conservatively means that she takes the largest expected payoff that is certain. Inequality (3) asserts that at least $v_A$ is certain, while (4) implies that no larger quantity can possibly be ensured. The theory we are developing concerns conservative play. This is already apparent from the content of FTMG and the use of the word "optimal" for the strategies $r'$ and $c'$. (The conservative nature of optimal strategies will be evident from a slightly different angle when we view them later as *minimax strategies*.)

In some games the strategies $r'$ and $c'$ of FTMG are not unique, even though the number $v_A$ must be. In the last example, for instance, $(1, 0, 0)$ is an additional optimal strategy for Colin. The uniqueness of $v_A$ is fully explained and proved in the following lemma. (The *existence* of $v_A$ lies much deeper.)

**Lemma 1.** *Suppose in addition to $v_A$, $r'$, and $c'$, related by (3) and (4), there exist a number $v_A^*$ and strategies $r^* \in \mathcal{S}_m$, $c^* \in \mathcal{S}_n$ such that*

$$E(r^*, c) \geq v_A^* \qquad \text{for all} \quad c \in \mathcal{S}_n, \tag{3*}$$

*and*

$$E(r, c^*) \leq v_A^* \qquad \textit{for all} \quad r \in \mathscr{S}_m. \tag{4*}$$

*Then* $v_A = v_A^*$.

*Proof.* As special cases of (3*) and (4*) we obtain

$$E(r^*, c') \geq v_A^*, \qquad E(r', c^*) \leq v_A^*.$$

But by (3) and (4),

$$E(r', c^*) \geq v_A, \qquad E(r^*, c') \leq v_A.$$

We deduce from the second and third of these four inequalities that $v_A \leq v_A^*$. On the other hand, the first and fourth inequalities imply that $v_A^* \leq v_A$. Hence $v_A = v_A^*$, as asserted. [It also now follows that $E(r^*, c^*) = E(r^*, c') = E(r', c^*) = E(r', c') = v_A$.] $\square$

We shall amply illustrate FTMG by examples, and ultimately prove it by LP theory. First, it is interesting and useful to observe that (3) and (4) are individually equivalent to seemingly weaker statements. Instead of checking (4), for example, for arbitrary $r \in \mathscr{S}_m$, it is sufficient to do so for only the following choices.

$$r^{(1)} = (1, 0, \ldots, 0),$$

$$r^{(2)} = (0, 1, \ldots, 0),$$

$$\vdots \qquad \vdots$$

$$r^{(m)} = (0, 0, \ldots, 1).$$

These strategies are called *Rose's pure strategies*, and Colin's pure strategies are analogously defined. Explicitly, we have

**Definition 5.** Given an $m \times n$ matrix game and any integer $h$ satisfying $1 \leq h \leq m$, let $r^{(h)}$ be that element of $\mathscr{S}_m$ defined by

$$r_i^{(h)} = \begin{cases} 1 & \text{if } i = h, \quad 1 \leq i \leq m, \\ 0 & \text{otherwise.} \end{cases} \tag{6}$$

Similarly for each $k$ $(1 \leq k \leq n)$, let $c^{(k)} \in \mathscr{S}_n$ be defined by

$$c_j^{(k)} = \begin{cases} 1 & \text{if } j = k \quad 1 \leq j \leq n, \\ 0 & \text{otherwise.} \end{cases} \tag{7}$$

Such elements of $\mathscr{S}_m$ and $\mathscr{S}_n$ are called *pure strategies*.

When $r$ and $c$ in (4) and (3) are restricted to pure strategies, simple and concrete inequalities result. Our Lemma 2 displays these inequalities and establishes their equivalence to (4) and (3). Lemmas 1 and 2 together imply that there can be only one number $v_A$ satisfying (III) and (IV) below.

**Lemma 2.** *Statements* (3) *and* (4) *of FTMG reduce to*

$$E(r', c^{(k)}) = \sum_{i=1}^{m} a_{ik} r'_i \geq v_A \quad \textit{for all} \quad k, \quad 1 \leq k \leq n \quad \text{(III)}$$

*and*

$$E(r^{(h)}, c') = \sum_{j=1}^{n} a_{hj} c'_j \leq v_A \quad \textit{for all} \quad h, \quad 1 \leq h \leq m, \quad \text{(IV)}$$

*respectively, when c and r range over pure strategies. Conversely,* (III) *implies* (3), *and* (IV) *implies* (4).

*Proof.* Assuming (3), we choose $k$ ($1 \leq k \leq n$), and then we choose $c = c^{(k)}$ in (3). We then obtain

$$\sum_{i=1}^{m} \sum_{j=1}^{n} a_{ij} r'_i c_j^{(k)} \geq v_A$$

from (3) and (2). By (7) all terms in the inner sum with $j \neq k$ vanish, and the remaining term is $a_{ik} r'_i$. Thus the last inequality reduces to the one in (III).

Conversely, assuming (III), let $c$ be an arbitrary element of $\mathscr{S}_n$. For each $k$, (III) yields

$$c_k \sum_{i=1}^{m} a_{ik} r'_i \geq c_k v_A.$$

Therefore,

$$\sum_{k=1}^{n} c_k \sum_{i=1}^{m} a_{ik} r'_i \geq \sum_{k=1}^{n} c_k v_A,$$

or

$$\sum_{i=1}^{m} \sum_{k=1}^{n} a_{ik} r'_i c_k \geq v_A,$$

as required for (3). Thus (3) and (III) are equivalent, and a similar argument proves the equivalence of (4) and (IV).  $\square$

It is convenient to record the following two definitions before we return to examples. The definitions take FTMG for granted before it is proved, but no logical problems will arise from this.

**Definition 6.** Given a matrix game $\Gamma_A$, the number $v_A$ in FTMG is called the *value* of the game. If $v_A = 0$, $\Gamma_A$ is called a *fair* game; if $v_A > 0$, $\Gamma_A$ *favors Rose*; if $v_A < 0$, $\Gamma_A$ *favors Colin.*

We shall see, for example, that Matching Pennies and Paper–Rock–Scissors are fair games. This is to be expected from the symmetry properties of the payoff matrices (see Problem 19). We shall also see that our initial $2 \times 3$ game favors Colin.

**Definition 7.** Any strategy $r'$ satisfying (3) or (III) is called an *optimal strategy for Rose*; a strategy $c'$ as in (4) or (IV) is an *optimal strategy for Colin*.

To continue illustrating FTMG, we again consider the example given for Definition 4. Here

$$A = \begin{bmatrix} 1 & -10 & 9 \\ 2 & 3 & 2 \\ 0 & 30 & -20 \end{bmatrix}.$$

We shall also use this example to elucidate "conservative" versus "speculative" play and to illustrate *saddle entries* of a payoff matrix.

The element $a_{21} = 2$ is *a minimum in its row and a maximum in its column*. As a consequence, we assert that $v_A = 2$, that $r' = (0, 1, 0) = r^{(2)}$ is an optimal strategy for Rose, and that $c' = (1, 0, 0) = c^{(1)}$ is an optimal strategy for Colin. To establish these assertions using Lemma 2 (and Lemma 1), we need only show

$$E(r', c^{(1)}), E(r', c^{(2)}), E(r', c^{(3)}) \geq 2 \tag{III}$$

and

$$E(r^{(1)}, c'), E(r^{(2)}, c'), E(r^{(3)}, c') \leq 2. \tag{IV}$$

These are immediately verified as follows:

$$
\begin{array}{ccc}
\begin{array}{ccc} 1 & 0 & 0 \end{array} & \begin{array}{ccc} 0 & 1 & 0 \end{array} & \begin{array}{ccc} 0 & 0 & 1 \end{array} \\
\begin{array}{c} 0 \\ 1 \\ 0 \end{array}\begin{bmatrix} 1 & -10 & 9 \\ 2 & 3 & 2 \\ 0 & 30 & -20 \end{bmatrix}, & \begin{array}{c} 0 \\ 1 \\ 0 \end{array}\begin{bmatrix} 1 & -10 & 9 \\ 2 & 3 & 2 \\ 0 & 30 & -20 \end{bmatrix}, & \begin{array}{c} 0 \\ 1 \\ 0 \end{array}\begin{bmatrix} 1 & -10 & 9 \\ 2 & 3 & 2 \\ 0 & 30 & -20 \end{bmatrix}; \quad \text{(III)} \\
E(r', c^{(1)}) = 2 & E(r', c^{(2)}) = 3 & E(r', c^{(3)}) = 2
\end{array}
$$

$$
\begin{array}{ccc}
\begin{array}{ccc} 1 & 0 & 0 \end{array} & \begin{array}{ccc} 1 & 0 & 0 \end{array} & \begin{array}{ccc} 1 & 0 & 0 \end{array} \\
\begin{array}{c} 1 \\ 0 \\ 0 \end{array}\begin{bmatrix} 1 & -10 & 9 \\ 2 & 3 & 2 \\ 0 & 30 & -20 \end{bmatrix}, & \begin{array}{c} 0 \\ 1 \\ 0 \end{array}\begin{bmatrix} 1 & -10 & 9 \\ 2 & 3 & 2 \\ 0 & 30 & -20 \end{bmatrix}, & \begin{array}{c} 0 \\ 0 \\ 1 \end{array}\begin{bmatrix} 1 & -10 & 9 \\ 2 & 3 & 2 \\ 0 & 30 & -20 \end{bmatrix}. \quad \text{(IV)} \\
E(r^{(1)}, c') = 1 & E(r^{(2)}, c') = 2 & E(r^{(3)}, c') = 0
\end{array}
$$

In particular, the game $\Gamma_A$ favors Rose (Definition 6). We remark (Problem 13) that Colin actually has infinitely many optimal strategies.

Before leaving this example let us suppose that Colin is dissatisfied with the implications of adopting his optimal strategy $c^{(1)}$. Attracted by the entry $-20$ in the third column, he might consider the strategy $c^{(3)}$. His hope would be that Rose adopts a strategy (not $r^{(2)}$) calling for the third row of $A$ to be played—the more often, the better. In view of the 30 dollar reward for Rose in the third row, this could be a reasonable hope. Below are a few illustrations with happy results for Colin:

$$
\begin{array}{ccc}
0 & 0 & 1
\end{array}
$$

$$
\begin{array}{c}
0 \\
0 \\
1
\end{array}
\left[
\begin{array}{ccc}
1 & -10 & 9 \\
2 & 3 & 2 \\
0 & 30 & -20
\end{array}
\right],
\qquad
\begin{array}{c}
0 \\
\frac{1}{2} \\
\frac{1}{2}
\end{array}
\left[
\begin{array}{ccc}
1 & -10 & 9 \\
2 & 3 & 2 \\
0 & 30 & -20
\end{array}
\right],
\qquad
\begin{array}{c}
\frac{1}{3} \\
\frac{1}{3} \\
\frac{1}{3}
\end{array}
\left[
\begin{array}{ccc}
1 & -10 & 9 \\
2 & 3 & 2 \\
0 & 30 & -20
\end{array}
\right].
$$

$$E(r, c^{(3)}) = -20 \qquad\qquad E(r, c^{(3)}) = -9 \qquad\qquad E(r, c^{(3)}) = -3$$

On the other hand, there is the risk that Rose will adopt a strategy combining unfavorably, from Colin's standpoint, with $c^{(3)}$. Examples are as follows:

$$
\begin{array}{ccc}
0 & 0 & 1
\end{array}
$$

$$
\begin{array}{c}
1 \\
0 \\
0
\end{array}
\left[
\begin{array}{ccc}
1 & -10 & 9 \\
2 & 3 & 2 \\
0 & 30 & -20
\end{array}
\right],
\qquad
\begin{array}{c}
\frac{1}{2} \\
\frac{1}{2} \\
0
\end{array}
\left[
\begin{array}{ccc}
1 & -10 & 9 \\
2 & 3 & 2 \\
0 & 30 & -20
\end{array}
\right].
$$

$$E(r, c^{(3)}) = 9 \qquad\qquad E(r, c^{(3)}) = \tfrac{11}{2}$$

   In summary, there are available to Colin strategies that, compared with his optimal strategy $c'$, offer both the possibility of greater gain and greater loss. Indeed, $0 \le E(r, c') \le 2$ for all $r \in \mathscr{S}_3$, whereas $E(r, c^{(3)})$ can range from $-20$ to 9. We cannot decide which strategy is "best" for Colin solely on the basis of a study of the function $E(r, c)$. Such a decision could depend on such factors as Colin's financial state or a prediction of the size of $r_3$ in the strategy Rose will adopt, or perhaps on other considerations beyond the scope of our discussion. We can only assert that, under the assumption that Colin wishes to play $\Gamma_A$ conservatively, he should select column one of $A$ with probability 1. He thereby limits his expected loss to (at most) 2 dollars.

   The game just discussed is very special in that pure optimal strategies exist. The cause of this phenomenon is the minimum–maximum property of the entry $a_{21}$. The following definition and theorem are suggested. The theorem establishes a special case of FTMG.

**Definition 8.** An element $a_{pq}$ of an $m \times n$ matrix $A$ is a *saddle entry* of $A$ if $a_{pq}$ is a minimum in its row and a maximum in its column. In symbols

$$a_{hq} \le a_{pq} \le a_{pk}, \qquad \text{for all } h, \quad 1 \le h \le m; \qquad \text{for all } k, \quad 1 \le k \le n. \quad (8)$$

**Theorem 1.** *Let $a_{pq}$ be a saddle entry in the $m \times n$ matrix $A$. Then FTMG holds for $\Gamma_A$, where $v_A = a_{pq}$, strategy $r^{(p)}$ is optimal for Rose, and strategy $c^{(q)}$ is optimal for Colin. Conversely, if FTMG holds with $r^{(p)}$ and $c^{(q)}$ as optimal strategies, then $a_{pq}$ is a saddle entry and $v_A = a_{pq}$.*

*Proof.* It is easy to see [from (2)] that $E(r^{(h)}, c^{(k)}) = a_{hk}$ for all $h$ and $k$ $(1 \le h \le m, 1 \le k \le n)$. Combining this observation with assumption (8) yields

$$E(r^{(p)}, c^{(k)}) \ge a_{pq} \qquad \text{for all } k, \quad 1 \le k \le n$$

and

$$E(r^{(h)}, c^{(q)}) \le a_{pq} \qquad \text{for all } h, \quad 1 \le h \le m.$$

By Lemma 2 (and also Lemma 1 on the uniqueness of $v_A$) all the desired conclusions follow.

Conversely, suppose $r^{(p)}$ and $c^{(q)}$ are optimal strategies in the game $\Gamma_A$. Definition 7 then gives

$$E(r^{(p)}, c^{(k)}) \ge v_A \qquad \text{for all } k, \quad 1 \le k \le n$$

and

$$E(r^{(h)}, c^{(q)}) \le v_A \qquad \text{for all } h, \quad 1 \le h \le m.$$

By the observation made above we conclude that $a_{hq} \le v_A \le a_{pk}$ for all $h$ and $k$. Choosing $h = p$ and $k = q$, we deduce $v_A = a_{pq}$ and therefore (8) (with $h$ and $k$ again arbitrary).   $\square$

A few final remarks before leaving the topic of saddle entries. A technique for finding all saddle entries, if any, of a given matrix is the following. First circle all row minima. For example,

$$\begin{bmatrix} -3 & \text{\textcircled{$-11$}} & -7 & -8 & -9 \\ \text{\textcircled{$-1$}} & 3 & \text{\textcircled{$-1$}} & \text{\textcircled{$-1$}} & 1 \\ \text{\textcircled{$-1$}} & 0 & \text{\textcircled{$-1$}} & \text{\textcircled{$-1$}} & \text{\textcircled{$-1$}} \\ -2 & 3 & -3 & -2 & \text{\textcircled{$-7$}} \end{bmatrix}.$$

Then circumscribe a square about any circled number that is a maximum in its column:

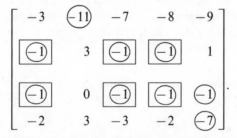

Any entry surrounded by both a circle and a square is a saddle entry, hence the six indicated $-1$'s. It is, of course, no accident that all the saddle entries are equal, for each must equal the value of the game based on the given matrix. Also, it is easy to prove such a statement directly, with no mention of game theorm (Problem 11).

In all of our introductory examples of matrix games there are no saddle entries. This is the "normal" or "nontrivial" situation. For instance for our $2 \times 3$ game and for Paper–Rock–Scissors the first step of our technique yields

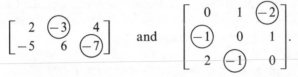

Since no circled number is a column maximum, no saddle entries exist.

For final illustrations of FTMG before its proof let us examine the two games of the preceding paragraph. We shall not yet use our ultimate LP method of finding game values and optimal strategies. Paper–Rock–Scissors is simple enough to admit an ad hoc analysis, while the $2 \times 3$ game is complex enough for us to be content with just verifying the correctness of optimal strategies "pulled out of a hat." (Actually, they are determined later by LP methods.)

For Paper–Rock–Scissors,

$$E(r, c) = r_1 c_2 - 2 r_1 c_3 - r_2 c_1 + r_2 c_3 + 2 r_3 c_1 - r_3 c_2$$

$$= (2 r_1 - r_2)(c_1 - c_3) + (2 c_1 - c_2)(r_3 - r_1).$$

If Rose chooses $r_1 = r_3$, and $r_2 = 2 r_1$, that is, $r' = (\frac{1}{4}, \frac{1}{2}, \frac{1}{4})$, then $E(r', c) = 0$ for all $c \in \mathscr{S}_3$. Similarly, for $c' = (\frac{1}{4}, \frac{1}{2}, \frac{1}{4})$, $E(r, c') = 0$ for all $r \in \mathscr{S}_3$. Hence (3) and (4) of FTMG hold with these strategies and with $v_A = 0$. A similar but easier analysis applied to Matching Pennies yields optimal strategies $r' = c' = (\frac{1}{2}, \frac{1}{2})$ and game value 0.

For the $2 \times 3$ game let us simply check that $r' = (\frac{11}{16}, \frac{5}{16})$ and $c' = (\frac{9}{16}, \frac{7}{16}, 0)$ are optimal strategies:

$$
\begin{array}{ccc}
\begin{array}{ccc} 1 & 0 & 0 \end{array} & \begin{array}{ccc} 0 & 1 & 0 \end{array} & \begin{array}{ccc} 0 & 0 & 1 \end{array} \\
\begin{array}{c} \frac{11}{16} \\ \frac{5}{16} \end{array}
\begin{bmatrix} 2 & -3 & 4 \\ -5 & 6 & -7 \end{bmatrix},
&
\begin{array}{c} \frac{11}{16} \\ \frac{5}{16} \end{array}
\begin{bmatrix} 2 & -3 & 4 \\ -5 & 6 & -7 \end{bmatrix},
&
\begin{array}{c} \frac{11}{16} \\ \frac{5}{16} \end{array}
\begin{bmatrix} 2 & -3 & 4 \\ -5 & 6 & -7 \end{bmatrix},
\\
E(r', c^{(1)}) = -\frac{3}{16} & E(r', c^{(2)}) = -\frac{3}{16} & E(r', c^{(3)}) = \frac{9}{16}
\end{array}
$$

$$
\begin{array}{cc}
\begin{array}{ccc} \frac{9}{16} & \frac{7}{16} & 0 \end{array} & \begin{array}{ccc} \frac{9}{16} & \frac{7}{16} & 0 \end{array} \\
\begin{array}{c} 1 \\ 0 \end{array}
\begin{bmatrix} 2 & -3 & 4 \\ -5 & 6 & -7 \end{bmatrix},
&
\begin{array}{c} 0 \\ 1 \end{array}
\begin{bmatrix} 2 & -3 & 4 \\ -5 & 6 & -7 \end{bmatrix}.
\\
E(r^{(1)}, c') = -\frac{3}{16} & E(r^{(2)}, c') = -\frac{3}{16}
\end{array}
$$

The check is complete and the value of this game is $-\frac{3}{16}$.

We now investigate the application of LP to matrix games. The discussion will culminate in a proof of FTMG and an elegant technique for computing game values and optimal strategies. Indeed, the value of any specific game, as well as optimal strategies for both players, can be found by solving a single one-phase LP problem. Moreover, this problem is particularly simple in form and immediately obtainable from the payoff matrix in question. There is just one minor drawback to these LP problems: Most games must be replaced by a closely related game before it is certain that the associated LP problem is applicable. The following lemma will be needed to transfer conclusions from the closely related game to the original game.

**Lemma 3.** *Let A be any matrix, let p be any number, and let the matrix B be related to A by*

$$b_{ij} = a_{ij} + p, \qquad for\ all\ i\ and\ j.$$

*Suppose FTMG holds for $\Gamma_B$. Then*

(i) *FTMG holds for $\Gamma_A$,*
(ii) *$v_B = v_A + p$,*
(iii) *$\Gamma_A$ and $\Gamma_B$ have the same optimal strategies for each of the two players.*

*Proof.* Let $A$ and $B$ have $m$ rows and $n$ columns. Then for any $r \in \mathscr{S}_m$ and $c \in \mathscr{S}_n$,

$$E_B(r, c) = \sum_{i=1}^{m} \sum_{j=1}^{n} b_{ij} r_i c_j = \sum_{i=1}^{m} \sum_{j=1}^{n} (a_{ij} + p) r_i c_j$$

$$= \sum_{i=1}^{m} \sum_{j=1}^{n} a_{ij} r_i c_j + p \sum_{i=1}^{m} \sum_{j=1}^{n} r_i c_j = E_A(r, c) + p.$$

Now, since FTMG holds for $\Gamma_B$, the value $v_B$ and optimal strategies $r'$ and $c'$ exist such that (analogs of) (3) and (4) hold. Specifically,

$$E_B(r, c') \le v_B \le E_B(r', c) \qquad for\ all\quad r \in \mathscr{S}_m, \quad c \in \mathscr{S}_n.$$

Hence, by the calculation above,

$$E_A(r, c') + p \le v_B \le E_A(r', c) + p,$$
$$E_A(r, c') \le v_B - p \le E_A(r', c) \qquad for\ all\quad r \in \mathscr{S}_m, \quad c \in \mathscr{S}_n.$$

Thus, the number $v_B - p$ satisfies the inequalities (3) and (4) required of $v_A$. By Lemma 1, there cannot be more than one such number. Hence FTMG holds for $\Gamma_A$ with $v_A = v_B - p$. We have now proved (i) and (ii). As for (iii), we have already shown that any optimal strategies $r'$ and $c'$ of the game $\Gamma_B$ are also optimal strategies of $\Gamma_A$. An almost identical argument establishes the converse, so we can consider the proof complete.    □

Next we define the special matrix games to which LP will be directly applied. It will be clear from Lemma 3 that all game-theoretic information can easily be transferred from these special games to arbitrary matrix games.

**Definition 9.** An $m \times n$ matrix $B$, or the corresponding matrix game $\Gamma_B$, has *property P* if every entry of $B$ is nonnegative and $B$ has no all-zero column.

In symbols,

(9)                 $b_{ij} \geq 0$     for all   $i$ and $j$,   $1 \leq i \leq m$,   $1 \leq j \leq n$

and

(10) For any $j$ $(1 \leq j \leq n)$, $\exists i$ $(1 \leq i \leq m)$ such that $b_{ij} > 0$.

For example, the matrix $\begin{bmatrix} 1 & -1 \\ -1 & 1 \end{bmatrix}$ of Matching Pennies does not have property $P$, but $\begin{bmatrix} 2 & 0 \\ 0 & 2 \end{bmatrix}$, obtained by adding 1 to every entry, does have property $P$. The matrices $\begin{bmatrix} -1 & 5 \\ -1 & 6 \end{bmatrix}$, $\begin{bmatrix} 0 & 6 \\ 0 & 9 \end{bmatrix}$ do not, the matrix $\begin{bmatrix} 1 & 7 \\ 1 & 8 \end{bmatrix}$ does. It is clear that any matrix can be transformed into one with property $P$ by adding a suitable positive number to each of its entries.

As final preparation for the proof of FTMG, we introduce the LP problems we shall employ. The proof requires, and we shall write down, a pair of dual LP problems. In applications to specific games, however, only the one in primal form need be considered. The relevance of these problems will become clear in Theorem 2 below.

**Definition 10.** Given an $m \times n$ matrix game $\Gamma_B$, *Colin's LP problem for $\Gamma_B$ is* the following.

$$(\text{CLP})_B: \quad \begin{cases} \text{Maximize} \quad f = \sum_{j=1}^{n} x_j \\ \text{subject to} \quad \sum_{j=1}^{n} b_{ij} x_j \leq 1, \qquad 1 \leq i \leq m \\ \qquad\qquad\qquad x_j \geq 0, \qquad 1 \leq j \leq n. \end{cases}$$

*Rose's LP problem for $\Gamma_B$ is the dual:*

$$(\text{RLP})_B: \quad \begin{cases} \text{Minimize} \quad g = \sum_{i=1}^{m} y_i \\ \text{subject to} \quad \sum_{i=1}^{m} b_{ij} y_i \geq 1, \qquad 1 \leq j \leq n \\ \qquad\qquad\qquad y_i \geq 0, \qquad 1 \leq i \leq m. \end{cases}$$

The symbol $y_i$ in this chapter assumes the function of the symbol $y_{n+i}$ of Chapter 5.

We remark that for arbitrary $B$, $(\text{CLP})_B$ is feasible. Indeed, $x_j = 0$ for $1 \leq j \leq n$ is clearly a feasible solution. A less obvious feasible solution, but one that will prove useful, is $x_j = \varepsilon$ $(1 \leq j \leq n)$, where $\varepsilon$ is positive and sufficiently small. Although feasible, the problem $(\text{CLP})_B$ need not have an OFS for arbitrary $B$. For instance, for the (unmodified) payoff matrix of Matching Pennies, $(\text{CLP})_B$ becomes

$$\begin{cases} \text{Maximize} \quad f = x_1 + x_2 \\ \text{subject to} \quad x_1 - x_2 \leq 1, \\ \qquad\qquad\quad -x_1 + x_2 \leq 1, \end{cases} \qquad x_1, x_2 \geq 0.$$

For $t > 0$, $(t, t)$ is feasible, while $f(t, t) = 2t \to +\infty$ as $t \to +\infty$. Thus this LP problem has no application to Matching Pennies. We mention in passing that $(\text{RLP})_B$ is infeasible for this choice of $B$, so this problem is also of no use.

Lemma 4 below shows that if $B$ has property $P$, the problem $(\text{CLP})_B$ must have an OFS (equivalently, $f$ must be bounded above). Afterward, Theorem 2 describes the theoretical importance and computational applications of $(\text{CLP})_B$ whenever an OFS exists.

**Lemma 4.** *If $B$ has property $P$, then $(\text{CLP})_B$ has an OFS.*

*Proof.* We have already observed that $(\text{CLP})_B$ is in any case feasible. We now use property $P$ to show that $f$ is bounded above on the feasible region. (The desired conclusion will then follow from Theorem 10 of Chapter 3.)

By (10) of Definition 9, $b_{i1} > 0$ for some $i$, $1 \le i \le m$. For this $i$ and for any feasible solution $(s_1, \ldots, s_n)$ of $(\text{CLP})_B$, the $i$th constraint gives $\sum_{j=1}^{n} b_{ij} s_j \le 1$. On the other hand, it follows from (9) of Definition 9 that $b_{i1} s_1 \le \sum_{j=1}^{n} b_{ij} s_j$. Therefore $s_1 \le 1/b_{i1}$. Thus there is an upper bound for the first components of feasible solutions. This holds similarly for the other components. The sum of these upper bounds is then an upper bound for the objective function $f$, as required. $\square$

We remark that property $P$ is sufficient but not necessary for $(\text{CLP})_B$ to have an OFS. Theorem 2 reveals that a necessary and sufficient condition for an OFS is that $\Gamma_B$ favors Rose. However, for specific games this condition can either fail to hold or be difficult to verify. Introducing property $P$ usually offers the most efficient way to analyze a matrix game by LP.

Before we state Theorem 2 it may be helpful to define *scalar multiplication* as it will appear in the theorem. Let $q$ be any positive integer and let $z$ be a $q$-tuple of real numbers: $z = (z_1, \ldots, z_q)$. Then for any real number $a$, the equation $w = az$ means that $w$ is the $q$-tuple such that $w_j = az_j$, $1 \le j \le q$.

**Theorem 2.** *For any matrix game $\Gamma_B$ the following two assertions are equivalent:*

(i)   *FTMG holds for $\Gamma_B$, and $v_B > 0$;*
(ii)  *$(\text{CLP})_B$ has an OFS.*

*Moreover, when (i) and (ii) hold, and we let*

$$u = \max f$$

*in $(\text{CLP})_B$, the following additional statements also hold:*

(iii)  *$u v_B = 1$;*
(iv)   *$c'$ is an optimal strategy for Colin if and only if $c' = (1/u)x'$ for some OFS $x'$ of $(\text{CLP})_B$;*
(v)    *$r'$ is an optimal strategy for Rose if and only if $r' = (1/u)y'$ for some OFS $y'$ of $(\text{RLP})_B$.*

*Proof.* Let us first assume (i). Then there are optimal strategies $c' \in \mathscr{S}_n$ and $r' \in \mathscr{S}_m$ such that

$$\sum_{j=1}^{n} b_{hj} c'_j \leq v_B, \qquad 1 \leq h \leq m, \tag{IV}$$

and

$$\sum_{i=1}^{m} b_{ik} r'_i \geq v_B, \qquad 1 \leq k \leq n. \tag{III}$$

[We are using (IV) and (III) of Lemma 2 with $B$ replacing $A$.] Since $v_B > 0$, we can divide (IV) by $v_B$ and obtain

$$\sum_{j=1}^{n} b_{hj} x'_j \leq 1, \qquad 1 \leq h \leq m,$$

where

$$x' = \frac{1}{v_B} c'.$$

Thus $x'$ is a feasible solution of $(\text{CLP})_B$. Similarly, dividing (III) by $v_B$ yields

$$\sum_{i=1}^{m} b_{ik} y'_i \geq 1, \qquad 1 \leq k \leq n,$$

where

$$y' = \frac{1}{v_B} r'.$$

Hence $y'$ is feasible for $(\text{RLP})_B$. Further,

$$f(x') = \sum_{j=1}^{n} x'_j = \sum_{j=1}^{n} \frac{c'_j}{v_B} = \frac{1}{v_B} = \sum_{i=1}^{m} \frac{r'_i}{v_B} = \sum_{i=1}^{m} y'_i = g(y').$$

Therefore, by Corollary 2 of Chapter 5, $f(x') = \max f$ and $g(y') = \min g$. Thus $x'$ and $y'$ are OFSs of $(\text{CLP})_B$ and $(\text{RLP})_B$, respectively. We have now shown that (i) implies (ii).

Conversely, suppose (ii) holds. Then, by the duality theorem, $(\text{RLP})_B$ also has an OFS. Let $x'$ and $y'$ be optimal for $(\text{CLP})_B$ and $(\text{RLP})_B$, respectively. Again by the duality theorem, if $u$ denotes $\max f$,

$$\sum_{j=1}^{n} x'_j = u = \sum_{i=1}^{m} y'_i.$$

Second, we have already noted that the $n$-tuple $(\varepsilon, \ldots, \varepsilon)$ is a feasible solution of $(\text{CLP})_B$ for suitable $\varepsilon > 0$. Hence

$$u \geq f(\varepsilon, \ldots, \varepsilon) = n\varepsilon > 0.$$

Therefore we can divide the inequalities

$$\sum_{j=1}^{n} b_{ij} x'_j \leq 1, \qquad 1 \leq i \leq m,$$

$$\sum_{i=1}^{m} b_{ij} y'_i \geq 1, \qquad 1 \leq j \leq n$$

(expressing the feasibility of $x'$ and $y'$) by $u$. This yields

$$\sum_{j=1}^{n} b_{ij} c'_j \leq \frac{1}{u}, \qquad 1 \leq i \leq m,$$

and

$$\sum_{i=1}^{m} b_{ij} r'_i \geq \frac{1}{u}, \qquad 1 \leq j \leq n,$$

where $c'$ and $r'$ are defined by

$$c' = \frac{1}{u} x', \qquad r' = \frac{1}{u} y'.$$

From $\sum x'_j = \sum y'_i = u$, it is clear that $c' \in \mathscr{S}_n$ and $r' \in \mathscr{S}_m$. We have therefore reached (IV) and (III) of Lemma 2 with optimal strategies $c'$ and $r'$, and with $v_B = 1/u$. Hence (i) is proved, and the equivalence of (i) and (ii) is established.

A review of the proof will easily reveal that (i) and (ii) imply (iii) through (v). For example, let us consider (iv). We have shown (in the first half of the proof) that, if $c'$ is an optimal strategy for Colin and if $x' = (1/v_B)c'$, then $x'$ is an OFS of $(CLP)_B$. Accepting (iii) as proved, we can write the last equation as $c' = (1/u)x'$, as required in (iv). The converse part of (iv) was established in the second half of the proof. $\square$

The combination of Lemma 3, Lemma 4, and Theorem 2 gives us an immediate proof of FTMG and an efficient algorithm for computing matrix game values and optimal strategies. Let us review and summarize.

*Proof of FTMG.* Let $\Gamma_A$ be an arbitrary matrix game. Define the matrix $B$ by

$$b_{ij} = a_{ij} + p, \qquad \text{for all } i \text{ and } j,$$

where $p$ is chosen so that $B$ has property $P$ (Definition 9). By Lemma 4, $(CLP)_B$ then has an OFS. Therefore, by Theorem 2, FTMG holds for $\Gamma_B$. Finally, by Lemma 3, FTMG also holds for $\Gamma_A$. $\square$

## Matrix Game–LP Algorithm

Given an arbitrary matrix game $\Gamma_A$, the following steps lead to the determination of $v_A$ and optimal strategies for both players. (Let $A$ be $m \times n$.)

(i) Add a number $p$ to every entry of $A$ so that the resulting matrix $B$ has property $P$.
(ii) Solve (the enlargement of) $(CLP)_B$ by SIMPLEX. With decision variables $x_1, \ldots, x_n$, slack variables $x_{n+1}, \ldots, x_{n+m}$, and objective function $F$, the

initial simplex tableau is the following:

|  | 1 | $\cdots$ | $n$ | |
|---|---|---|---|---|
| $n + 1$ | $b_{11}$ | $\cdots$ | $b_{1n}$ | 1 |
| $\vdots$ | $\vdots$ | | $\vdots$ | $\vdots$ |
| $n + m$ | $b_{m1}$ | $\cdots$ | $b_{mn}$ | 1 |
| $F$ | $-1$ | $\cdots$ | $-1$ | 0 |

From the final simplex tableau read off an OFS of $(CLP)_B$, an OFS of the dual problem (as explained in connection with the duality theorem), and max $f$. Let these be denoted by $x' = (x'_1, \ldots, x'_n)$, $y' = (y'_1, \ldots, y'_m)$, and $u$, respectively.

(iii) Let $c' = (1/u)x'$, $r' = (1/u)y'$. Then

$c'$ is an optimal strategy for Colin.
$r'$ is an optimal strategy for Rose.
$v_A = v_B - p = 1/u - p$.

Occasionally, students forget step (i) and apply SIMPLEX to $(CLP)_A$. By Theorem 2 all will be well if $v_A > 0$. Otherwise, $f$ will prove to be unbounded. In (i) and elsewhere $p$ can be chosen with the simple requirement that $a_{ij} + p > 0$ for all $i$ and $j$; this is easier to describe than property $P$. The latter, however, usually permits the matrix $B$ to have one or more zeros whose presence can simplify computations. To see this, the reader is asked in Problem 23 to analyze Matching Pennies with both

$$\begin{bmatrix} 2 & 0 \\ 0 & 2 \end{bmatrix} \quad \text{and} \quad \begin{bmatrix} 3 & 1 \\ 1 & 3 \end{bmatrix}$$

as choices for $B$ in (i). Finally, before illustrating the Matrix Game–LP Algorithm, we remind the reader that games with a saddle entry are easily analyzed without LP.

Let us now apply our algorithm to $\Gamma_A$ with

$$A = \begin{bmatrix} 2 & -3 & 4 \\ -5 & 6 & -7 \end{bmatrix}.$$

(i) Let $p = 7$. Then

$$B = \begin{bmatrix} 9 & 4 & 11 \\ 2 & 13 & 0 \end{bmatrix}.$$

(ii) The main part of the algorithm follows:

|  | 1 | 2 | 3 | |
|---|---|---|---|---|
| 4 | 9 | 4 | 11 | 1 |
| 5 | 2 | ⑬ | 0 | 1 |
| $F$ | $-1$ | $-1$ | $-1$ | 0 |

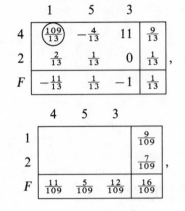

$$x' = (\tfrac{9}{109}, \tfrac{7}{109}, 0), \qquad y' = (\tfrac{11}{109}, \tfrac{5}{109}), \qquad u = \tfrac{16}{109}.$$

(iii) In conclusion,

$$c' = \tfrac{109}{16}x' = (\tfrac{9}{16}, \tfrac{7}{16}, 0),$$

$$r' = \tfrac{109}{16}y' = (\tfrac{11}{16}, \tfrac{5}{16}),$$

$$v_A = v_B - 7 = \tfrac{109}{16} - 7 = -\tfrac{3}{16}.$$

These results were discussed and verified earlier.

Our final topic is an alternative description of optimal strategies. The new description, like our original definition, will suggest a conservative or cautious approach to playing matrix games. For definiteness we shall concentrate on the selection of a strategy for Colin. The selection can be conceived in two steps:

(i) Find the worst consequence—from Colin's standpoint—of every strategy available to Colin.

(ii) Find a strategy whose worst consequence is as good as possible for Colin.

We begin by clarifying step (i). Let $c$ be an arbitrary strategy adoptable by Colin. (Throughout our discussion, $c$ denotes a strategy for Colin; $r$, a strategy for Rose.) Once Colin adopts strategy $c$, $E(r, c)$ becomes a function only of $r$. More precisely, to each strategy $c$ there corresponds a uniquely determined function $r \to E(r, c)$. The worst consequence, for Colin, of adopting the strategy $c$ is that Rose will adopt a strategy maximizing this function. (We show later that this function does indeed have a maximum.) Now, the maximum value of the function $r \to E(r, c)$ is denoted $\max_r E(r, c)$. The symbol $\max_r$ is read "maximum over $r$" or "maximum over all $r$." Such phrases indicate that we consider all choices of $r$, and no other choices, in determining the maximum of the expression following $\max_r$. Using this notation, we can say that the worst consequence of Colin's adopting an arbitrary strategy $c$ is that Rose's expected payoff will be $\max_r E(r, c)$.

Before going on to step (ii) we illustrate step (i) by means of the game

Matching Pennies:

$$r_1 \begin{bmatrix} 1 & -1 \\ -1 & 1 \end{bmatrix}, \qquad E(r, c) = (r_1 - r_2)(c_1 - c_2).$$

For arbitrary $c$, there are three cases:

(i) $c_1 - c_2 > 0$,
(ii) $c_1 - c_2 < 0$,
(iii) $c_1 = c_2$.

In case (i), $E(r, c)$ is largest if $r_1 = 1$ and $r_2 = 0$. Thus

$$\max_r E(r, c) = E(r^{(1)}, c) = c_1 - c_2.$$

In case (ii), $E(r, c)$ is largest if $r_1 = 0$ and $r_2 = 1$. Then

$$\max_r E(r, c) = E(r^{(2)}, c) = -(c_1 - c_2).$$

Hence, in all cases, including (iii),

$$\max_r E(r, c) = |c_1 - c_2|.$$

In this example, and indeed in general, $\max_r E(r, c)$ is a function of $c$. Precisely, each strategy $c$ determines a function $r \to E(r, c)$, and each such function in turn determines a maximum value, $\max_r E(r, c)$. Therefore, there is a function $c \to \max_r E(r, c)$. This brings us to step (ii). The meaning of this step is the following: Determine a strategy *minimizing* the function $c \to \max_r E(r, c)$. (The existence of a minimum value will be demonstrated below.) For Matching Pennies, it is clear from the last paragraph that $(\frac{1}{2}, \frac{1}{2})$ is such a minimizing strategy. Anticipating our general result, we recall that $(\frac{1}{2}, \frac{1}{2})$ is also Colin's optimal strategy (as in Definition 7).

In general, step (ii) demands a strategy $c'$ for which

$$\max_r E(r, c') \leq \max_r E(r, c) \qquad \text{for all } c.$$

We shall need to formulate this in one other way. In accordance with our earlier comments on notation, the minimum value of the function $c \to \max_r E(r, c)$ is denoted $\min_c[\max_r E(r, c)]$. But if $c'$ is as just described, the minimum value of this function is also $\max_r E(r, c')$. Therefore

$$\max_r E(r, c') = \min_c \left[ \max_r E(r, c) \right].$$

The expression on the right has inspired the term *minimax strategy* for the strategy $c'$. The main goals of this discussion are to show that minimax strategies are precisely the same as optimal strategies for Colin, to establish an analogous result for Rose, and to prove that

$$\min_c \left[ \max_r E(r, c) \right] = \max_r \left[ \min_c E(r, c) \right] = v_A.$$

All of this is accomplished by the following theorem, the "minimax theorem."

**Theorem 3.** *For any matrix game* $\Gamma_A$, *all the maxima and minima specified below exist, and the following assertions hold*:

(i) $c'$ *is an optimal strategy for Colin if and only if*

$$\max_r E(r, c') = \min_c \left[ \max_r E(r, c) \right];$$

(ii) $r'$ *is an optimal strategy for Rose if and only if*

$$\min_c E(r', c) = \max_r \left[ \min_c E(r, c) \right];$$

(iii) $\qquad \max_r \left[ \min_c E(r, c) \right] = v_A = \min_c \left[ \max_r E(r, c) \right].$

*Proof.* Let $A$ be $m \times n$. We first show that for any (fixed) $c$, $\max_r E(r, c)$ exists. Here and throughout the theorem, $r$ denotes an element of $\mathscr{S}_m$, and $c$ an element of $\mathscr{S}_n$. For each $r$,

$$E(r, c) = \sum_{i=1}^m r_i \sum_{j=1}^n a_{ij} c_j = \sum_{i=1}^m r_i \gamma_i,$$

where

$$\gamma_i = \sum_{j=1}^n a_{ij} c_j, \qquad 1 \le i \le m.$$

Let $1 \le h \le m$ with

$$\gamma_h = \max_{1 \le i \le m} \gamma_i.$$

(The maximum of *finitely* many real numbers always exists.)

Then, for the pure strategy $r^{(h)}$,

$$E(r^{(h)}, c) = \sum_{i=1}^m r_i^{(h)} \gamma_i = \gamma_h.$$

On the other hand, for arbitrary $r$,

$$E(r, c) = \sum_{i=1}^m r_i \gamma_i \le \sum_{i=1}^m r_i \gamma_h = \gamma_h.$$

Thus

$$\max_r E(r, c) = \gamma_h.$$

Similarly, for any $r$, $\min_c E(r, c)$ exists.

Now let $r'$ and $c'$ be any optimal strategies for Rose and Colin respectively. Then the existence and values of $\max_r E(r, c')$ and $\min_c E(r', c)$ are more simply discussed. For instance, since [by (4)] $E(r, c') \leq v_A$ for every $r$, while [by (5)] $E(r', c') = v_A$, it follows at once that

$$v_A = \max_r E(r, c').$$

(Conversely, it is clear that if a strategy $c'$ satisfies this equation, then $c'$ satisfies the definition of an optimal strategy for Colin.) Next for any $c$, (3) gives

$$v_A \leq E(r', c) \leq \max_r E(r, c).$$

Therefore

$$\max_r E(r, c') \leq \max_r E(r, c), \qquad \text{for all } c.$$

But this statement is precisely equivalent to the equation in (i). Moreover, the right-hand equation of (iii) now immediately follows.

Similarly, by (3) and (5)

$$v_A = \min_c E(r', c),$$

while by (4)

$$\min_c E(r, c) \leq E(r, c') \leq v_A.$$

Hence

$$\min_c E(r, c) \leq \min_c E(r', c), \qquad \text{for all } r.$$

This establishes the equation in (ii) and with it the remaining equation in (iii).

The converse parts of (i) and (ii) are now immediate. For instance, if $c'$ is a strategy satisfying the equation in (i), we use the second equation in (iii) to conclude $\max_r E(r, c') = v_A$. As observed above, this makes $c'$ an optimal strategy for Colin. A similar argument finishes (ii), and the proof is complete.    □

We have, of course, used FTMG and our definitions of $v_A$ and optimal strategies in proving Theorem 3. Alternatively, one could first prove

$$\max_r \left[ \min_c E(r, c) \right] = \min_c \left[ \max_r E(r, c) \right],$$

then define $v_A$ to be the common value of these two expressions, and then define optimal strategies $c'$ and $r'$ by the equations in (i) and (ii). One now has all the equations of (i) through (iii), and our inequalities (3) and (4) immediately follow, as in the last paragraph of the proof.

In general, "$\max_r$" and "$\min_c$" do not "commute." For instance,

$$\max_{0 \leq r \leq 1} \left[ \min_{0 \leq c \leq 1} (r - c)^2 \right] = 0,$$

whereas

$$\min_{0 \le c \le 1} \left[ \max_{0 \le r \le 1} (r - c)^2 \right] = \tfrac{1}{4}.$$

Here $r$ and $c$ range over $\mathscr{S}_1$, but $(r - c)^2$ is not of the correct form for $E(r, c)$. A hint for proving these two equations is given in Problem 26.

In conclusion, our discussion has described in a new way the conservative nature of optimal strategies. We can now say that the goal of the conservative column player is to minimize $\max_r E(r, c)$, his opponent's maximum expected payoff. Analogously, the conservative row player seeks to maximize $\min_c E(r, c)$. Our Matrix Game–LP Algorithm provides the means for both players to achieve their objectives.

## PROBLEMS

1. The game with payoff matrix

$$A = \begin{bmatrix} 5 & -1 \\ -1 & 1 \end{bmatrix}$$

   is a variation of Matching Pennies in which Rose wins 5 dollars if both players choose heads. Show that

   $$E(r, c) = \tfrac{1}{2}(r_1 + r_2)(c_1 + c_2) + \tfrac{1}{2}(3r_1 - r_2)(3c_1 - c_2).$$

2. Use the last equation to find a strategy for Rose that reduces $E(r, c)$ to a constant as $c$ varies over $\mathscr{S}_2$. What is the constant? Do the analogous task for Colin. Show from the relevant definitions that you have found $v_A$ and optimal strategies for both players.

3. Your grade in a college course is a *weighted average* of your exam grades. (If the latter are $e_1, \ldots, e_n$, a weighted average is a number of the form $\sum_{k=1}^{n} c_k e_k$, where $c \in \mathscr{S}_n$.) All your exam grades are at least 80. Prove that your grade in the course is also at least 80. To see what this has to do with game theory, show that

   $$E(r, c) = \sum_{k=1}^{n} c_k E(r, c^{(k)}),$$

   and review the statement of Lemma 2. (Recall that $c^{(k)}$ is Colin's $k$th pure strategy.)

4. In Problems 4 through 7, $A$ is an $m \times n$ matrix and

   $$m(r) = \min \left\{ \sum_{i=1}^{m} a_{ij} r_i : j = 1, \ldots, n \right\},$$

   $$M(c) = \max \left\{ \sum_{j=1}^{n} a_{ij} c_j : i = 1, \ldots, m \right\},$$

   for each $r \in \mathscr{S}_m$ and $c \in \mathscr{S}_n$. [Certain knowledgeable readers will readily grasp $m(r)$ as the minimum *dot product* of $r$ with the various columns of $A$, and analogously for $M(c)$.] Test your understanding of these two expressions by showing that

$m(r) = -\frac{3}{4}$ and $M(c) = 1$ in the example

$$\begin{array}{c} \phantom{\frac{3}{4}} \quad \frac{1}{3} \quad \frac{1}{3} \quad \frac{1}{3} \\ \frac{3}{4}\left[\begin{array}{ccc} 2 & -3 & 4 \\ \frac{1}{4} \\ -5 & 6 & -7 \end{array}\right]. \end{array}$$

5. Prove the identity

$$\sum_{i=1}^{m} r_i \left[ M(c) - \sum_{j=1}^{n} a_{ij}c_j \right] + \sum_{j=1}^{n} c_j \left[ \sum_{i=1}^{m} a_{ij}r_i - m(r) \right] = M(c) - m(r)$$

(to be important in Problem 7). Observe that the quantities in square brackets are nonnegative and, therefore, that $m(r) \le M(c)$.

6. Show that strategies $r$ and $c$ are simultaneously optimal (for Rose and Colin, respectively) if and only if $m(r) = M(c)$.
   Hint: If both are optimal, show from the relevant definitions that $M(c) \le v_A \le m(r)$. Then use the inequality of the preceding problem. Conversely, if $m(r) = M(c)$, note that this number and the strategies $r$ and $c$ satisfy the requirements for the game value and optimal strategies, respectively.

7. Use results of Problems 5 and 6 to prove that $r$ and $c$ are simultaneously optimal if and only if both of the following statements hold:
   (i) For all $i$, either $r_i = 0$ or $\sum_{j=1}^{n} a_{ij}c_j = M(c)$.
   (ii) For all $j$, either $c_j = 0$ or $\sum_{i=1}^{m} a_{ij}r_i = m(r)$.

8. Verify (i) and (ii) in the following three examples:

$$\begin{array}{c} \phantom{x} \quad 1 \quad 0 \\ \begin{array}{c} 1 \\ 0 \end{array}\left[\begin{array}{cc} 0 & 1 \\ -1 & 0 \end{array}\right], \end{array} \qquad \begin{array}{c} \frac{9}{16} \quad \frac{7}{16} \quad 0 \\ \begin{array}{c} \frac{11}{16} \\ \frac{5}{16} \end{array}\left[\begin{array}{ccc} 2 & -3 & 4 \\ -5 & 6 & -7 \end{array}\right], \qquad \begin{array}{c} \frac{2}{5} \quad \frac{3}{5} \\ \begin{array}{c} 0 \\ 1 \\ 0 \end{array}\left[\begin{array}{ccc} -3 & 2 \\ 0 & 0 \\ 1 & -4 \end{array}\right]. \end{array} \end{array}$$

In the third example there is an instance in which "either or" is actually "both."

9. In general, if $r$ and $c$ are optimal, then (i) and (ii) of Problem 7 hold with $M(c)$ and $m(r)$ both replaced by $v_A$. The converse, however, is false.
   Hint: Consider the first payoff matrix in Problem 8 together with the strategies $r = c = (0, 1)$. (This combination also gives an example in which $E(r, c) = v_A$, but neither $r$ nor $c$ is optimal.)

10. Given that $(0, \frac{1}{5}, \frac{4}{5})$ is an optimal strategy for Rose if

$$A = \left[\begin{array}{ccc} 5 & -1 & -2 \\ 13 & 2 & -7 \\ -2 & 1 & 3 \end{array}\right],$$

use the "sufficiency" of (i) and (ii) to find an optimal strategy for Colin.

11. Suppose $a_{pq}$ and $a_{rs}$ are saddle entries of a matrix $A$. Prove without any game theory that $a_{pq} = a_{rs}$.
    Hint: Begin by comparing the sizes of $a_{pq}, a_{ps},$ and $a_{rs}$.

12. Find $v_A$ and optimal strategies for both players if

$$A = \begin{bmatrix} 3 & -1 & -1 & 14 & -3 \\ 5 & 9 & 5 & 11 & 13 \\ 2 & 6 & 0 & 5 & 6 \\ 4 & 9 & 3 & 4 & -1 \end{bmatrix}.$$

13. For the game of the text with payoff matrix

$$A = \begin{bmatrix} 1 & -10 & 9 \\ 2 & 3 & 2 \\ 0 & 30 & -20 \end{bmatrix},$$

show that a strategy $(c_1, c_2, c_3)$ is optimal for Colin if and only if $c_2 = 0$ and $c_1 \geq \frac{7}{8}$.

The optimal strategies found in this problem can be written $(\frac{7}{8} + \frac{1}{8}t, 0, \frac{1}{8} - \frac{1}{8}t)$, where $0 \leq t \leq 1$. Readers familiar with scalar multiplication and vector addition will see that this triple is equal to

$$t(1, 0, 0) + (1 - t)(\tfrac{7}{8}, 0, \tfrac{1}{8}), \qquad 0 \leq t \leq 1.$$

Recall that the strategies $(1, 0, 0)$ and $(\frac{7}{8}, 0, \frac{1}{8})$ were found to be optimal in the text. It is true, in general, that such a combination (a *convex combination*) of optimal strategies is also optimal. Readers with certain additional knowledge will observe that $(1, 0, 0)$ and $(\frac{7}{8}, 0, \frac{1}{8})$ are *extreme points* of the set of Colin's optimal strategies. In general, to obtain all optimal strategies it is sufficient to find the extreme optimal strategies.

14. If

$$A = \begin{bmatrix} 0 & -100 \\ 0 & 1 \end{bmatrix},$$

does Rose have an optimal strategy that uses the first row (has nonzero first component)? State your reaction to the following argument that she does not have such an optimal strategy: Rose has nothing to gain and 100 dollars to lose by playing the first row, whereas she has nothing to lose and 1 dollar to gain by playing the second row.

15. (Dominance) Suppose the first row of a payoff matrix $A$ is dominated by the second, entry by entry: $a_{1j} \leq a_{2j}$ for $j = 1, \dots, n$. Let

$$A_1 = \begin{bmatrix} a_{21} & \cdots & a_{2n} \\ \vdots & & \vdots \\ a_{m1} & \cdots & a_{mn} \end{bmatrix},$$

the matrix obtained from $A$ by removing the first row. Suppose $(r_2, \dots, r_m)$ and $(c_1, \dots, c_n)$ are optimal strategies for the respective players in the game $\Gamma_{A_1}$. Show that $(0, r_2, \dots, r_m)$ and $(c_1, \dots, c_n)$ are optimal in $\Gamma_A$, and that $v_A = v_{A_1}$.

16. Use the results (and the assumption) of Problem 15 to formulate a 3-step *dominance algorithm*:

   (i) Discard $A$ in favor of a smaller payoff matrix.
   (ii) Analyze the smaller game.
   (iii) Transfer conclusions from the smaller game to the original game.

   Transform these rough instructions into precise ones. Note that your algorithm has one drawback: It can lose optimal strategies for Rose. For examples, consider the game in Problem 14 and the game with matrix $\begin{bmatrix} 0 & \frac{1}{2} \\ 0 & 2 \end{bmatrix}$. In the latter game, Rose has an optimal strategy in which the dominated first row is selected with probability 1!

17. Formulate a dominance theorem for two *arbitrary* rows and then for two arbitrary *columns*. Apply yours theorems repeatedly to

$$A = \begin{bmatrix} 5 & -8 & 4 & 5 & -9 \\ 4 & 2 & 0 & -3 & 4 \\ 3 & -6 & 9 & 6 & -8 \\ 2 & -5 & 7 & 6 & -7 \end{bmatrix}$$

   until you reach a payoff matrix treated in the text. Find $v_A$ and optimal strategies for Rose and Colin.

   *Answer*: $-\frac{3}{16}$, $(0, \frac{11}{16}, 0, \frac{5}{16})$, and $(0, \frac{9}{16}, 0, \frac{7}{16}, 0)$.

18. The matrix

$$A = \begin{bmatrix} 5 & -1 & 0 \\ -1 & 1 & 1 \\ 1 & -1 & -5 \end{bmatrix}$$

   possesses a certain amount of symmetry between positive and negative payoffs. (Compare the first row and the third column, and observe the remaining $2 \times 2$ submatrix.) Do you think $\Gamma_A$ is a fair game? Investigate using dominance.

19. A certain symmetry property that a *square* matrix $A$ can possess implies that $v_A = 0$, and that Rose and Colin have exactly the same optimal strategies. (We need FTMG for the existence of $v_A$.) Each of the following matrices has the property that *its set of rows is the same as the set of "negatives" of its columns*:

$$\begin{bmatrix} 1 & -1 \\ -1 & 1 \end{bmatrix}, \qquad \begin{bmatrix} 0 & 1 & -2 \\ -1 & 0 & 1 \\ 2 & -1 & 0 \end{bmatrix}, \qquad \begin{bmatrix} 2 & -2 & 5 & -7 \\ -2 & 2 & -7 & 5 \\ 7 & -5 & 8 & -8 \\ -5 & 7 & -8 & 8 \end{bmatrix},$$

$a_{1v} = -a_{v2},$         $a_{1v} = -a_{v1},$         $a_{1v} = -a_{v2},$

$a_{2v} = -a_{v1},$         $a_{2v} = -a_{v2},$         $a_{2v} = -a_{v1},$

$(v = 1, 2)$         $a_{3v} = -a_{v3},$         $a_{3v} = -a_{v4},$

                     $(v = 1, 2, 3)$         $a_{4v} = -a_{v3},$

                                             $(v = 1, 2, 3, 4).$

Suppose $A$ is any $n \times n$ matrix with this property, and $r$ and $c$ are optimal strategies for the respective players. Fill in the details of the following proof that $r$ is an optimal strategy *for Colin*, that $c$ is an optimal strategy *for Rose*, and that $v_A = 0$.

For arbitrary $i$ $(i = 1, \ldots, n)$, there is a $k$ $(k = 1, \ldots, n)$ such that $a_{iv} = -a_{vk}$ $(v = 1, \ldots, n)$. Then $\sum_{v=1}^{n} a_{vk} r_v \geq v_A$. Therefore $\sum_{v=1}^{n} a_{iv} r_v \leq -v_A$. Similarly, for arbitrary $j$, $\sum_{v=1}^{n} a_{vj} c_v \geq -v_A$. The last two conclusions imply all the stated assertions.

20. Apply Problem 19 and the simple theorem below to show that the games with matrices

$$
\begin{bmatrix} -a & 0 & c \\ 0 & a & -b \\ b & -c & 0 \end{bmatrix},
\qquad
\begin{bmatrix} 6 & -1 & 1 & -3 \\ -8 & 3 & -6 & 8 \\ -3 & 1 & -1 & 6 \\ 8 & -6 & 3 & -8 \end{bmatrix}
$$

are fair. Let $\tilde{A}$ be a payoff matrix obtained from a matrix $A$ by interchanging the first and second rows. Prove the following three statements:

(i) $(r_1, r_2, \ldots, r_m)$ is an optimal strategy for Rose in $\Gamma_A$ if and only if $(r_2, r_1, \ldots, r_m)$ is such in $\Gamma_{\tilde{A}}$.

(ii) Colin has the same optimal strategies in both games.

(iii) $v_{\tilde{A}} = v_A$.

21. Consider the game with payoff matrix

$$
\begin{bmatrix} 0 & a & -b \\ -a & 0 & c \\ b & -c & 0 \end{bmatrix}.
$$

(i) Explain why $(x, y, z)$ is an optimal strategy for both players if all the following conditions are satisfied.

$$
ay - bz = 0,
$$
$$
-ax \qquad + cz = 0,
$$
$$
bx - cy \qquad = 0, \qquad x, y, z \geq 0.
$$
$$
x + y + z = 1,
$$

(ii) Show that these conditions can all be met if $a$, $b$, and $c$, are all positive and thereby obtain the desired strategy.

(iii) Find optimal strategies if $a > 0$, $b < 0$, and $c > 0$.

22. Show in any way you can that the games with matrices

$$
\begin{bmatrix} 5 & -4 & 0 \\ -1 & 1 & 4 \\ 1 & -1 & -5 \end{bmatrix},
\qquad
\begin{bmatrix} 5 & -6 & 0 \\ -1 & 1 & 6 \\ 1 & -1 & -5 \end{bmatrix},
$$

are unfair and fair, respectively.

23. Apply the Matrix Game–LP Algorithm to Matching Pennies in two different ways: First add 1 to every entry of the payoff matrix, and then add 2.

24. Use LP to analyze the game with payoff matrix

$$A = \begin{bmatrix} -2 & 1 & 0 \\ 3 & -4 & 2 \end{bmatrix}.$$

Answer: $v_A = -\frac{1}{2}$, $r = (\frac{7}{10}, \frac{3}{10})$, $c = (\frac{1}{2}, \frac{1}{2}, 0)$.

25. Let the payoff matrix of a game be $m \times n$ with $m < n$ (as in the previous problem). Prove that Colin has an optimal strategy with at least $n - m$ zero components.

26. This problem demonstrates that $\max_r$ and $\min_c$ need not commute outside the context of matrix games. Prove that for $0 \le r \le 1$ and $0 \le c \le 1$,

(i)
$$\max_r \left[ \min_c (r - c)^2 \right] = 0,$$

but

(ii)
$$\min_c \left[ \max_r (r - c)^2 \right] = \frac{1}{4}.$$

Hint: For (i), show that the function of $r$ being maximized is identically zero. For (ii), begin by showing that

$$\max_r (r - c)^2 = \begin{cases} (1 - c)^2 & \text{for} \quad 0 \le c \le \frac{1}{2}, \\ c^2 & \text{for} \quad \frac{1}{2} \le c \le 1. \end{cases}$$

27. The result of the last problem, though negative in character, illustrates a generally true statement. Let $X$ and $Y$ be any two sets, and let $f: X \times Y \to \mathbf{R}$. (Given any $x \in X$ and $y \in Y$, a real number $f(x, y)$ is determined.) Prove that

$$\max_x \left[ \min_y f(x, y) \right] \le \min_y \left[ \max_x f(x, y) \right],$$

assuming that all the maxima and minima exist.

Hint: Let $x_0 \in X$ with $\max_x[\min_y f(x, y)] = \min_y f(x_0, y)$. Similarly, let $y_0 \in Y$ with $\min_y[\max_x f(x, y)] = \max_x f(x, y_0)$. It remains only to show that $\min_y f(x_0, y) \le \max_x f(x, y_0)$.

# Bibliography

1. Beale, E.M.L., Cycling in the dual simplex algorithm, *Naval Res. Logist. Quart.*, **2** (1955), 269–275.
2. Bland, R.G., New finite pivoting rules for the simplex method, *Math. Oper. Res.*, **2** (1977), 103–107.
3. Chvátal, V., *Linear Programming*, Freeman, New York, 1983.
4. Dantzig, G.B., *Linear Programming and Extensions*, Princeton University Press, Princeton, NJ, 1963.

# Index

## Undergraduate Texts in Mathematics

*(continued)*

**Simmonds:** A Brief on Tensor Analysis.

**Singer/Thorpe:** Lecture Notes on Elementary Topology and Geometry.

**Smith:** Linear Algebra. Second edition.

**Smith:** Primer of Modern Analysis.

**Stanton/White:** Constructive Combinatorics.

**Thorpe:** Elementary Topics in Differential Geometry.

**Troutman:** Variational Calculus with Elementary Convexity.

**Wilson:** Much Ado About Calculus.